## THE TRANSCRIPTS

# CHINESE SAYINGS
## BOOK 1

### LASZLO MONTGOMERY

Chinese Sayings Book 1

By Laszlo Montgomery

Trade Paper: 978-988-8843-98-5
Digital: 978-988-8843-99-2

© 2024 Laszlo Montgomery

HISTORY / Asia / China

EB225

All rights reserved. No part of this book may be reproduced in material form, by any means, whether graphic, electronic, mechanical or other, including photocopying or information storage, in whole or in part. May not be used to prepare other publications without written permission from the publisher except in the case of brief quotations embodied in critical articles or reviews. For information contact info@earnshawbooks.com

Published in Hong Kong by Earnshaw Books Ltd.

# CONTENTS

Author's Forward — IX

**Episode 1 Take care in that melon field** — 1
瓜田李下—Guā Tián Lǐ Xià

**Episode 2 Fen-wise and Yuan-foolish** — 7
贪小失大—Tān Xiǎo Shī Dà

**Episode 3 A Lousy Place to Fish** — 15
缘木求鱼—Yuán Mù Qiú Yú

**Episode 4 Should I Save or Should I Throw** — 21
味如鸡肋—Wèi Rú Jī Lèi

**Episode 5 The Entourage** — 27
鸡鸣狗盗—Jī Míng Gǒu Dào

**Episode 6 The Hu and the Hu** — 35
狐假虎威—Hú Jiǎ Hǔ Wēi

**Episode 7 Too Rich for my Blood** — 41
曲高和寡—Qǔ Gāo Hè Guǎ

**Episode 8 Surrounded!** — 47
四面楚歌—Sì Miàn Chǔ Gē

**Episode 9 A Man of Great Inability** — 55
滥竽充数—Làn Yú Chōng Shù

**Episode 10 True to his Word** — 61
完璧归赵—Wán Bì Guī Zhào

**Episode 11 So Sorry!**     **69**
负荆请罪—Fù Jīng Qǐng Zuì

**Episode 12 Go For Broke**     **75**
破釜沉舟—Pò Fǔ Chén Zhōu

**Episode 13 A Man of Great Ambition**     **83**
鸿鹄之志—Hóng Hú Zhī Zhì

**Episode 14 He sure had a lot of gall**     **89**
卧薪尝胆—Wò Xīn Cháng Dǎn

**Episode 15 Gotta get to the gym**     **97**
髀肉复生—Bì Ròu Fù Shēng

**Episode 16 The Four-Legged Snake**     **103**
画蛇添足—Huà Shé Tiān Zú

**Episode 17 That's Worth a Lot**     **111**
价值连城—Jià Zhí Lián Chéng

**Episode 18 One bad apple**     **119**
害群之马—Hài Qún Zhī Mǎ

**Episode 19 Rejected!**     **125**
虎口余生—Hǔ Kǒu Yu Sheng

**Episode 20 Mr. Know It All**     **139**
井底之蛙—Jǐng Dǐ Zhī Wā

**Episode 21 Mom of the Millennia**     **147**
孟母三迁—Mèng Mǔ Sān Qiān

**Episode 22 Produced by the gods**     **153**
神工鬼斧—Shén Gōng Guǐ Fǔ

**Episode 23    A Horse is a Horse, Of Course, Of Course**    159
指鹿为马—Zhǐ Lù Wéi Mǎ

**Episode 24 Looks Good on Paper**    167
纸上谈兵—Zhǐ Shàng Tán Bīng

**Episode 25 Putting out the fire with gasoline**    177
抱薪救火—Bào Xīn Jiù Huǒ

**Episode 26 What's the Rush?**    183
揠苗助长—Yà Miáo Zhù Zhǎng

**Episode 27 Mirror, Mirror on the wall**    189
门庭若市—Mén Tíng Ruò Shì

**Episode 28 Locked and Loaded**    197
厉兵秣马—Lì Bīng Mò Mǎ

**Episode 29 I Should Have Known Better**    205
借箸代筹—Jiè Zhù Dài Chóu

**Episode 30 Wouldn't Change a Thing**    215
一字千金—Yī Zì Qiān Jīn

# AUTHOR'S FORWARD

Ever since I began my Chinese studies back in 1979, I fell in love with Chinese "chengyu" idioms. These were kinds of traditional idiomatic expression that were usually, but not always, made up of four characters.

What made them particularly enjoyable to learn about was that they were derived from ancient and medieval classical literature, and stories rooted in history. Even though many of them were more than two thousand years old, they were still widely used in modern Chinese to convey something on the one hand complex but on the other hand somewhat profound. They were concise yet memorable.

One of the aspects of these Chinese Sayings was that their figurative meaning almost always could not be deduced simply by reading the four (or more) characters.

About five years after I launched the China History Podcast, I thought that with these "chengyu" phrases so often rooted in history, why not launch a new podcast show that would introduce one chengyu per episode. Whatever the origins of the idiom, be it a work of literature, folklore, official history, historical events, or philosophical text.

What's cool about these chengyu or Chinese Sayings is that they conveyed rich meanings, morals, and pearls of wisdom in a compact form, often summarizing a story or a moral lesson. Chengyu phrases added depth and nuance to the language.

Since I launched the Chinese Sayings Podcast, over 90 episodes have been produced as of the summer of 2024. Both Cathay Pacific and Singapore Airlines carry these Chinese Sayings Podcast shows in their inflight entertainment systems.

In these anthologies being published by Earnshaw Books, the entirety of these famous and historic Chinese Sayings will be presented in three volumes. Each will consist of my curated selections of the most engaging, relatable, and thought-provoking Chengyu-Chinese Sayings. No matter if you're a fluent Chinese speaker, in the process of learning or never studied before, these books will introduce you to a wonderful slice of Chinese culture that you can use in your daily life, at home, at the office, or out with your friends and family.

Here in Volume 1 of this 3-Part Chinese Sayings Anthology, chengyu idioms from the Warring States and Han Dynasty will be featured. I hope you will enjoy and appreciate these cultural classics from more than two thousand years ago.

Laszlo Montgomery

## Chinese Sayings Book 1
### Episode 1

---

## TAKE CARE IN THAT MELON FIELD

瓜田李下—Guā Tián Lǐ Xià

In the inaugural episode of the Chinese Sayings Podcast, Laszlo introduces one of his favorites from his earliest days: Guā Tián Li Xià. 瓜田李下. This one goes all the way back to the early days of the Three Kingdoms Period. The lesson it teaches us is to watch yourself when you're in circumstances that might possibly be misunderstood and show you in a suspicious light.

## TRANSCRIPT

00:00　　Hi everyone, Laszlo Montgomery here. This episode is the first in a series that will introduce you, Chinese speaker or non-Chinese speaker, to the interesting and amusing world of Chinese sayings. I thought I'd kick off the series with one of my personal favorite sayings. I came across this one back during the early Reagan years right after I began my Chinese studies. This one isn't terribly well-known but it's a very nice textbook example of how some of these Chinese idioms and proverbs work. And if I may say so, I've used this one quite a bit over the decades.

00:40　　As I explained in the introduction, standing on their own, it's hard to tell what some of these seemingly meaningless phrases are all about. But if you know the backstory, suddenly it becomes crystal clear what's up with that saying.

00:57 Like most of these *chengyu* or idioms, this one's only four syllables long. Guātián Lǐxià. Four Chinese characters.

01:20 A guā is a melon, just a generic term for any kind of melon. Tián is a field. So a Guātián is a melon field.

Lǐ is a character that can be a number of things. It's the character for most of the people with the Lǐ surname. A lǐ is also a plum and that's what it means in this case, specifically a plum tree.

Xià, the final character, means underneath or below.

So, say these four characters real fast and you get Guātián Lǐxià.

Melon field - Under a plum tree.

Hmmm, must be a story behind that one.

01:52 Indeed there is, otherwise this whole podcast series would lack a main point. The story behind Melon field-Under a plum tree goes back to the second century, the period of the Eastern Han Dynasty in China. The clock is ticking down on this dynasty and it will come to an end in the year 220.

02:14 The origin of this Saying comes from a poem called The Song of the Gentleman. *Jūnzǐ Xíng* 君子行. Contained in

CHINESE SAYINGS BOOK 1
EPISODE 1

the lines of this poem were the words:

*Jūnzǐ fáng wèirán, bù chù xiányí jiān, guātián bù nà lǚ, lǐ xià bùzhèng guān.*

君子防未然，不处嫌疑间。
瓜田不纳履，李下不正冠。

02:38   Ahhh, so what does that mean? A *Jūnzǐ* is a gentleman, *fáng wèirán* in order to prevent, *bù chù xiányí jiān*, anything looking suspicious. *Guātián bù nà lǚ* never ties his shoes in a melon field. Nor does he ever *lǐ xià bùzhèng guān*, adjusts his hat under a plum tree.

03:06   If you're in someone's melon field and you see your laces are untied, for god's sake wait until you're out of the field before you tie them. Otherwise someone might see you from a distance and wonder, hmmm what's that guy doing kneeling down in that melon field? Is he stealing from that farmer?

03:25   And if you're chilling under a plum tree, waiting for someone perhaps, don't go fiddling with your hat. If someone sees you with your arms up in the air underneath a plum tree they might misconstrue your actions and think you're stealing fruit.

03:41   The Song of the Gentleman, from which this chengyu example is derived, came from someone you maybe never heard of. His name was Cáo Zhí 曹植. He was quite a celebrated man of letters and his father is one of the giants of ancient Chinese history and I would

# CHINESE SAYINGS BOOK 1
# EPISODE 1

dare to say might make the shortlist of the top ten best known Chinese leaders of all time. This was Cáo Cāo 曹操. He was the chancellor during the last dozen years of the Eastern Han and the most powerful military man and political figure in China at the time. Cáo Cāo used his military might and control of the Han emperors to enhance his legitimacy.

**04:21** In his poem, Cáo Zhí teaches us that a gentleman should exercise proper judgement at all times and never allow himself to be observed in circumstances that might be considered of a suspicious nature. He teaches that a gentleman should conduct himself always in such a way that no matter where he is or what he's doing, no one's gonna look suspiciously on him and wonder, hmmmmmm, what's up with that guy.... what's he doing over there?

**04:54** So when you're trying to tell someone don't get caught in suspicious circumstances, just say to them Hey, *guātián lǐxià*. Melon Field, Under a Plum Tree. And because now you're all now properly schooled about Cáo Zhí's story, you hold the key that unlocks the meaning behind this seemingly meaningless phrase, "melon field, under a plum tree."

*Guātián Lǐxià* ladies and gentlemen.

**05:22** So, keep that in mind. Not just gentlemen, everyone. Don't put yourself in a situation where you're potentially suspect. You may be found guilty without even committing the offense. Don't put yourself in a

CHINESE SAYINGS BOOK 1
EPISODE 1

|       | position where people might call you a shady character. |
|-------|---|
| 05:38 | It's not as bad as getting caught with your hand in the cookie jar, but in a melon field, under a plum tree kinda situation you definitely might have your hand on the lid. |
| 05:50 | So, that's our CSP for this time, the Chinese Sayings Podcast. If you found it to your liking, come back for more next time. I'll be offering you up another pearl of wisdom from China's ancient philosophers, warriors, writers, statesmen and kings that, thousands of years later still resonates in our modern 21st century world. |
| 06:14 | Until next time me little beauties, this is Laszlo Montgomery signing off from hot and sunny fantastic LA. Again I invite you to listen to our other shows, the venerable and long-running China History Podcast and the delectable Tea History Podcast, available in your podcast app of choice or at the website at teacup dot media. Do consider coming back next time for another delicious and satisfying episode of the Chinese Sayings Podcast. |

# Chinese Sayings Book 1
# Episode 2

**THE TRANSCRIPTS**

## FEN-WISE AND YUAN-FOOLISH

贪小失大—Tān Xiǎo Shī Dà

In this episode, Laszlo introduces a story from the early 4th Century BCE, the Warring States period that preceded the unification of China under Qin Shihuang. It concerns the ruler down in the southwest kingdom of Shu, centered around Chengdu. Thanks to his greediness for a small gift, he ended up losing big later on. He was so busy counting his pennies earned in a quick score that he lost sight of the pounds he'd lose down the road. This ruler's moment of weakness was immortalized by Lü Buwei in his highly respected Lü Shi Chunqiu who called him out as one who Tan Xiao Shi Da.

## TRANSCRIPT

**00:00** Hi everyone, Laszlo Montgomery back again with another Chinese saying for your repertoire. Thanks for giving the Chinese Sayings Podcast another shot.

**00:13** This saying today is even older than last episode's. This time we're traveling back in time to more than twenty-three centuries ago, to the year 316 BCE. In the West, while our story is taking place, Classical Greek civilization is at its peak and Alexander the Great had perished only seven years prior at the Palace of Nebuchadnezzar in Babylon.

## CHINESE SAYINGS BOOK 1
## EPISODE 2

**00:34** And in China, still no unified country exists yet called China. There's only a collection of warring states trying to annihilate each other so that one could emerge victorious as ruler of the land. In 316 BCE, when this story takes place, it still hadn't been done.

**00:54** 4th Century BCE. Before the Common Era. All the dates I'm mentioning in this episode will be BCE.

**01:02** Our Chinese Saying, *chengyu*, for today goes back to the time of King Huìwén of Qin 秦惠文. He was the ancestor of the Qin Emperor who unified China and built that amazing mausoleum in Xian with all its terracotta warriors and horses. Our story behind this chengyu comes straight from the China History Podcast episode 158... The Rise and Fall of the Qin Part 2. CHP listeners might remember the Shíniú Dào, the Stone Cattle Road that cut through the Qínlǐng Mountains that separated Shǎnxī and Sìchuān Provinces.

**01:43** Yeah, today's story looks at the not too bright ruler down in the ancient state of Shǔ who, thanks to his short-sightedness goes down in Chinese history as the man who gave us a staple among popular chengyu, Tān Xiǎo Shī dà.

Allow me to explain how that one works. Four characters.

Tān means to covet or be greedy for something.

Xiǎo means small.

CHINESE SAYINGS BOOK 1
EPISODE 2

So Tān Xiǎo means you are greedy for small things.

Shī means to lose.

And Dà means great or big.

Shī dà, to lose big.

02:5 Tān Xiǎo Shī dà, because you are greedy for the small thing, you end up losing the big thing. This is one of those sayings where you might be able to figure out the meaning of the chengyu just by translating the individual characters. But the back story to this one is particularly good, so let's see what it is.

02:47 If you're familiar with the Qín State or you have already listened to the China History Podcast series on the Rise and Fall of the Qin, you'll recall they had a lot of big ideas about conquering the various kingdoms to their east. But before they went after those big strong guys, they had their eyes on lesser states that they believed should be taken first in order to enhance their army, bring additional wealth into the Qin State to fortify it and allow them to bulk up enough to go take on these other more powerful states.

03:22 So King Huìwén and his advisors agreed they had to start with these two kingdoms to the south, Bā and Shǔ, down where Sichuan is today. Now, this is just a legend. One of King Huìwén's advisors had told him that they should create a ruse that took advantage of the Shǔ ruler's well-known avaricious ways. He had a soft spot

# CHINESE SAYINGS BOOK 1
# EPISODE 2

for gold, silver and other kinds of tangible treasure.

**03:52** Just as an aside, this land of Bā and Shǔ was the location of the mysterious and ancient Sānxīngduī and Jīnshā Culture. This was all fun and around the capital city of Chéngdū. Bā state was more to the east where Chóngqìng is today.

**04:14** The Qín had sent out exploratory missions to see how they could get a big enough army down there to take this kingdom down. What they found was that the Qínlǐng Mountains presented too big an obstacle for marching an army through to the south. It was passable by individuals on foot, but for the kind of military plans they had in mind, it wasn't feasible.

**04:36** So someone came up with the idea to create these carved stone cattle, five of them in all, and they filled the extremities of the animal with pieces of gold. They knew, the ruler in that part of China that we'd know as Sichuan Province wouldn't be able to resist such a gift. And they sent someone down to Shǔ, on a goodwill mission by all appearances, with a list of all these valuable gifts the Qín ruler wanted to present to the King, or actually his title was the Marquis of Shǔ. This ruler thereupon sent envoys to Qín to go check these gifts out and they were amazed with these stone cattle or Shíniú that were actually filled with gold.

**05:24** Well, this Marquis of Shǔ had an advisor who had more wisdom and common sense than his boss. And this advisor warned his superior not to be fooled. He

CHINESE SAYINGS BOOK 1
EPISODE 2

probably hadn't heard about the Trojans from about a century before, but this was the general idea of what he was telling the Shǔ ruler. He warned that these men of Qín were up to something. Their reputation as a fighting machine was already well-known around town and he told the king, don't accept this gift and don't let them come down to Shǔ. You'll never be able to get rid of them.

06:01 This Marquis of Shǔ fulminated over the benefits and risks and decided to ignore his wise minister and went ahead and gave instructions to invite these Qin ambassadors down to Shǔ to present their gifts. The Qin ambassador told the Shǔ ruler's people that a road was gonna need to be built in order to facilitate convenient transport of these stone cattle through the Qínlǐng Mountains that separated Qin from Shǔ.

06:29 The Shǔ ruler must have considered the building of this road a small price to pay and at once arranged for a sufficient number of workers to go and start quarrying enough limestone out of the hills to build a road that could facilitate easy transport of these big heavy gifts through the mountains. This road became known as the Shíniú Dào, the Stone Cattle Road. There may be bits and pieces of this road that still exist today.

06:59 You can probably guess what happened. After the road was finished and after the gifts had been presented, the Qín army later on just marched down all the way to present day Chéngdū and put an end to this Shǔ State in 316 BCE. And the Bā State next door. And that spelled

11

the end of Bā-Shǔ and that whole incredible civilization, again, in what is today Sichuan Province.

07:28   So almost a hundred years after the Qin army put an end to the Bā-Shǔ kingdoms, around 239 BCE, Lǚ Bùwéi 吕不韦, another famous name from those times, also prominently mentioned in that China History Podcast episode on the rise and fall of the Qin, wrote this history of the times called the Lǚ Shì Chūnqiū, The Spring and Autumn Annals of Master Lǚ.

07:53   And it was Lǚ Bùwéi who remarked that this Shǔ Ruler, because he coveted something as small and insignificant as a little gold, later on, ended up losing his whole kingdom. Because he tān xiǎo, coveted the small, he ended up shī dà, losing the big. So this is where Tān Xiǎo Shī Dà came from.

08:19   And this *chengyu* has been used for a couple thousand years since whenever a similar situation arises where someone loses out big because they were too greedy for the small gain that came their way first.

08:35   Tān Xiǎo Shī Dà. Don't lose sight of the big picture for the sake of a quick score. This is the Chinese version of our "penny wise and pound foolish." Someone who watches the pennies they spend but not the pounds.

08:50   There's also a variation of this Saying that goes Yīn Xiǎo Shī Dà 因小失大, substituting the word Yīn, which means "because" instead of Tān which means to covet or be greedy for. Yīn Xiǎo Shī Dà. Because of the small you

# CHINESE SAYINGS BOOK 1
# EPISODE 2

lose the big. Same meaning

**09:07** So that's the *chengyu* for this time. Don't forget there's more going on at Teacup Media than this Chinese Sayings Podcast. For almost three hundred hours of the greatest hits ever from Chinese history, go check the China History Podcast. And while you're at it, pour yourself a cuppa and enjoy The Tea History Podcast. You won't regret that, I guarantee it.

**09:31** Until the next time, on behalf of the whole gang at Teacup Media, management, the interns, hangers on, and Apple Scruffs, this is Laszlo Montgomery signing off from an undisclosed location west of the San Andreas Fault here in Southern California. Think about joining me next time, won't you, for another interesting and useful episode of the Chinese Sayings Podcast.

# Chinese Sayings Book 1
# Episode 3

## A LOUSY PLACE TO FISH

缘木求鱼—Yuán Mù Qiú Yú

## TRANSCRIPT

**00:00** — Hey everyone I'm back again with another Chinese Sayings Podcast. Laszlo Montgomery here, as usual. Another good one today, a staple again if I may add. I've heard and read this one more than a few times in my checkered career. To Climb a Tree to Catch a Fish. You can probably guess this *chengyu* has something to do with attempting to achieve something that's quite impossible.

**00:26** — Four characters. Yuán Mù Qiú Yú. Climb a tree to catch a fish.

Here is the breakdown of these four syllables.

**00:36** — Yuán, a character with several meanings, none of which seem to have anything to do with climbing. But that's what it means in this example.

And Mù means wood or tree.

# CHINESE SAYINGS BOOK 1
# EPISODE 3

So Yuán Mù in this case means to climb a tree.

Qiú means to seek or look for.

And Yú means fish.

Qiú yú, to seek a fish.

Yuán Mù, climb a tree.

Qiú Yú, look for a fish.

**01:05** To climb a tree to catch a fish. And like all these *chengyu* presented to you at The Chinese Sayings Podcast, there's a story behind this. And without any further delay that might put us into stoppage time later, let me get on with it.

**01:20** The story of Climb a Tree to Catch a Fish goes all the way back to the Warring States Period again, the Zhōu Dynasty. I mentioned before the Zhou Dynasty was divided up between the Western and Eastern Zhou. And the Eastern Zhou was further divided up between the Spring and Autumn period followed by the Warring States period. This was the dynasty that witnessed the birth of core Chinese culture. This was the dynasty where the foundation was poured.

**01:57** It was a very fascinating time in ancient Chinese history. This was China's period equivalent to Europe's Medieval period with castles, fiefdoms, nobles and knights in white satin.

CHINESE SAYINGS BOOK 1
EPISODE 3

02:09 | And the most famous guy to come out of that period by a landslide was Confucius. And Confucius's most famous follower back in the day was Mencius. In China, they know him as Mèngzǐ. Mèngzǐ's time on the good earth was from 372 to 289 BCE, 2,300 years ago. And no surprise that this chéngyǔ come straight out of his eponymous book called The Mèngzǐ.

02:39 | This was the Warring States period in China.

02:41 | China in those days, late 4th century, early 3rd century BCE time, was still all divided up into difference states. There were a lot of them, but in the time we're talking about today there were less than ten.

02:56 | And one of those states was the State of Qí in present-day Shāndōng province.

03:03 | The ruler there at the time when Mèngzǐ walked the earth was King Xuān of Qi 齐宣王. And this king had grand designs on all the lands in China and seemed determined to conquer everyone by force of arms.

03:17 | Mèngzǐ was also from the state of Qí and he was contemporary to this Qí King Xuān. And Mèngzǐ was a regular visitor to the King who called Mèngzǐ to the palace often to seek his sagacious advice.

03:33 | Mèngzǐ's main argument to the King, when he was told of King Xuān's big plans to conquer the world, was that he should consider a more benevolent path to leadership instead. If he led through benevolence and wisdom

CHINESE SAYINGS BOOK 1
EPISODE 3

people, from other lands would flock to him and accept his leadership and authority based on the goodness he exhibited.

03:56   This King Xuān of Qí was looking for a faster route to power. He was already making plans to conquer the states adjacent to him. But his real end game was to take over the world, which in those days meant China.

04:11   Mèngzǐ tried to talk him out of this and asked him, did he not have enough treasure and money? The best food whenever he wanted it? Works of priceless art hanging in his palace, enough royal robes in his wardrobe, not enough people at his beck and call 24 hours a day? What is it that made him so unsatisfied with his current lot in life? What more did he want that he didn't already have.

04:39   King Xuān said, all those material things are meaningless. That's not what he was after.

04:45   So Mèngzǐ just looked at him and he concluded that this royal was just trying to take over the whole world for no other reason than to have everyone bow to him.

04:56   Mengzi chided him, that to do something like this militarily was like climbing a tree to catch a fish.

The King looked at Mèngzǐ and asked is it really that hopeless? Like Climbing a tree to catch a fish?

05:10   Mèngzǐ said it's worse than that. If you climb a tree but don't catch any fish, no big deal. You tried something

CHINESE SAYINGS BOOK 1
EPISODE 3

that was impossible but nobody got hurt. But if you try and conquer the world through force of arms you'll bring calamity on yourself, your house and your kingdom. How are you, one single kingdom, going to take out the other eight kingdoms? You're not even the most powerful. He told King Xuān, it's always the strong kingdoms who defeat the weaker ones and those with many soldiers who defeat those with too few. He plainly told his king, if you try to carry out your grand scheme you're guaranteed to fail.

05:53  And with advice like that, good King Xuān of Qí reconsidered and decided to back-burner his plans.

05:59  So climbing a tree to catch a fish means you're wasting your time trying to do the impossible. You're totally going about it the wrong way. You're not gonna get what you want. Yuán Mù Qiú Yú. You're climbing a tree to catch a fish. And we all know, fish don't live in trees.

06:16  So this is another nice example of how Chinese chengyu works. Four character phrase and has a nice historic backstory to it with a nice moral. Yuán Mù Qiú Yú. To climb a tree to catch a fish. Thank you, Mengzi, for such profundity.

06:35  Okay, that's going to be it for this time. This is Laszlo Montgomery signing off from LA and saying stay out of the trees if you're looking to catch fish. Thanks a million for listening, and I cordially welcome every single one of you to go check out our brother and sister podcasts at Teacup dot media. The China History Podcast and

CHINESE SAYINGS BOOK 1
EPISODE 3

the Tea History Podcast. Everything, all in one place for your inconvenience at Teacup.media. You won't be sorry.

07:04 | Take care everyone and please be my guest next time for another delectable episode of the Chinese Sayings Podcast.

 **Chinese Sayings Book 1 Episode 4**

**THE TRANSCRIPTS**

## SHOULD I SAVE OR SHOULD I THROW

味如鸡肋—Wèi Rú Jī Lèi

## TRANSCRIPT

00:00 | Greetings one and all, Laszlo Montgomery again bringing you another satisfying and nutritious Chinese Saying. This time I picked out another, well, easy to pronounce classic that goes back to the last years of the Eastern Han. And anytime you talk about the end of the Han Dynasty you know Cáo Cāo is going to get a mention. He's the star of our Chengyu today, our Chinese Saying.

00:26 | This story comes to us courtesy of the Book of Wèi in the Sān Guó Zhì 三国志, the Records of the Three Kingdoms, the most authoritative historical source that has made it down to us in the 21st Century. This would have been one of Luó Guànzhōng's 罗贯中 primary sources when he wrote his classic novel, *Romance of the Three Kingdoms*.

00:48 | Today we look at Wèi Rú Jī Lèi, four syllables, standard equipment when it comes to these chengyu.

Here's the blow-by-blow analysis:

CHINESE SAYINGS BOOK 1
EPISODE 4

Wèi means taste, the taste of something.

Rú means like, as, or as if.

Combine the two characters and you have Wèi Rú, the taste is like or this tastes as if.....

Moving right along, Jī is a chicken.

and Lèi means ribs.

Jī lèi, chicken ribs.

**01:22** Tastes like chicken ribs. Wèi Rú Jī Lèi . Okay, well that doesn't appear to have any obvious meaning so there has to be a story behind it, involving Cáo Cāo.

**01:35** He lived from 155 to 220. Cáo Cāo was chancellor during the final years of the Eastern Han Dynasty. After he died, his son Cáo Pī, went and founded the Kingdom of Wèi and ruled as their first emperor. They were one of the Three Kingdoms who fought to win control of a unified China.

**01:56** After the death of the final Hàn emperor, that was it as far as the unified country called China. Now the Middle Kingdom was divvied up into three separate Kingdoms called Wèi, Shǔ and Wú. Again the details long ago presented in the China History Podcast.

**02:18** Our story behind Wèi Rú Jī Lèi takes place in Shǎnxī Province, mainly around the city of Hànzhōng 汉中. I

CHINESE SAYINGS BOOK 1
EPISODE 4

don't mean to keep dropping these little nugs on you about little-known facts but Hànzhōng is the city that gave us the name of the Han Dynasty since Liú Bāng was formerly King of Hànzhōng. After Liú Bāng did away with Xiàng Yǔ at the end of the Chǔ Hàn Contention he named his new dynasty the Hàn, from Hànzhōng.

02:50   Cáo Cāo first took this city in 215 from Liú Bèi of Shǔ. This Shǔ Kingdom was in the southwest, around Sichuan. After Cáo Cāo took Hànzhōng away from them, Liú Bèi's troops retreated back to their home base in Sichuan. After he felt that Hànzhōng was under control, Cáo Cāo felt it was safe for him to head back to his base in Yèchéng 邺城, an ancient district in Hebei, present-day Línzhāng County 临漳县.

03:21   After Cáo Cāo left Hànzhōng, the Shǔ ruler Liú Bèi began to make plans to take the city back. In the fall of 218, he did just that. He took the city and after pushing Cáo Cāo's army out of Hànzhōng, he moved in and assumed control. Cáo Cāo wasn't happy about this and put his generals on notice to take it back. But it was to no avail. After trying a few times, and real hard I might add, Cáo Cāo's army couldn't extract Liú Bèi and his Shǔ army from Hànzhōng. Every battle fought ended without a decisive result. No one could defeat the other.

04:02   Finally in September 218, Cáo Cāo had had enough with his generals excuses, so he pushed them all aside and rode back to Hànzhōng and said he himself would lead the army against the Shǔ Kingdom of Liú Bèi. But even after throwing everything he had against Liú Bèi and his

## CHINESE SAYINGS BOOK 1
## EPISODE 4

army, Cáo Cāo couldn't declare a total victory. This was really demoralizing. And so one day, when things were not looking good, Cáo Cāo retired to his tent to have his evening rice and ponder his next move. Keep at it? Or declare victory and head home.

**04:42** While Cáo Cāo sat there, contemplating his options, one of his generals entered the tent as he did every night at this time to get the master password.

According to the story, as he fulminated over what the new password should be, Cáo Cāo stared down at his bowl of soup and replied, "Chicken Ribs."

**05:04** The general bowed and exited the tent and passed the word through the chain of command. Finally the password was given to Yáng Xiū 杨修, perhaps Cáo Cāo's most trusted right hand man.

**05:17** Upon hearing the new password, and knowing his boss like he did, Yáng Xiū immediately gave the orders to his subordinates to quietly begin making preparations to withdraw from Hànzhōng.

**05:31** The general asked Yáng Xiū, how could he possibly know this was going to be Cáo Cāo's command? Yáng Xiū told him plainly that this password from Cáo Cāo was all he needed to know about where the King of Wèi's head was.

**05:46** Yáng Xiū further said the situation had become desperate and hopeless. Provisions were running out. The Shǔ

CHINESE SAYINGS BOOK 1
EPISODE 4

military turned out to be stronger than they expected. By using a password such as chicken ribs, Cáo Cāo was revealing what was in his heart. Yáng Xiū continued. You see, chicken ribs are tasteless and not much use. But tasteless as they may be, they got a little bit of meat on the bone that makes it a pity to throw them away. That is what Hànzhōng has become to Cáo Cāo. It wasn't life or death to take and hold the city, but what a shame to walk away without it.

**06:28** Sure enough the next morning, bright and early, Cáo Cāo issued the order to withdraw from Hànzhōng.

**06:36** And from this, we get Wèi Rú Jī Lèi. Tastes like chicken ribs, meaning something of little value or use, yet just enough value or use whereby to give it up would seem a waste. It can also mean, to lack interest in doing something because to do it yields almost nothing to your benefit. It also can be used to describe anything in your life that might be called rubbish but which you can't bring yourself to toss in the garbage. Wèi Rú Jī Lèi.

**07:09** Cáo Cāo was thinking he had to take Hànzhōng back but after expending so much blood and treasure to accomplish the task he realized, what is he trying so hard for? It wasn't worth it.

**07:23** I'm sure we all have plenty of chicken ribs hanging around our house and in our fridge. You know it's not really worth it to keep it but why throw it away? That ratty sofa you might have in your home or office, the edges of which your cats have clawed to shreds. You know you should dump it, but it's still comfortable and serves its purpose. What a shame to toss it. A nice example of chicken ribs.

**07:50** So that's the story of Cáo Cāo, Liú Bèi, Yáng Xiū and the chicken ribs. Wèi Rú Jī Lèi. Not much use but a pity to toss it.

**08:00** For more about all these guys, remember, the China History Podcast is available for you 24/7 with all the major details about this and other topics from the thousands of years of Chinese history. All free, all the time.

**08:15** And don't forget, if you're traveling on Cathay Pacific Airways, you can listen to this Chinese Sayings Podcast and the China History Podcast. One more reason to fly CX.

**08:26** Thanks everyone, Laszlo Montgomery, on behalf of the entire staff and management here at Teacup Media, signing off from Los Angeles, California. Consider joining me next time for another Chinese Sayings Podcast. Take care everyone!

# Chinese Sayings Book 1
# Episode 5

## THE ENTOURAGE

鸡鸣狗盗—Jī Míng Gǒu Dào

A noble lord accepts an ill-fated job offer and relies on his entourage to extricate him from his situation.

## TRANSCRIPT

00:00 | Hey everyone, welcome back to the Chinese Sayings Podcast. Laszlo Montgomery here, once again, with yet another good one for you. This Chinese saying has a very excellent pedigree, coming from no less a source than the Shǐ Jì itself, the Records of the Grand Historian, Sīmǎ Qiān's magnum opus and monument to his father Sīmǎ Tán.

00:24 | Today we will look at the story behind Jīmíng Gǒudào.

00:29 | As usual, the story came from ancient times. Four characters, four syllables, thrown together with no apparent meaning? I'd say this one is about as typical a chengyu as you can get.

Jīmíng Gǒudào.

# CHINESE SAYINGS BOOK 1
# EPISODE 5

Here's the molecular breakdown.

A Jī? That's a chicken or rooster.

Míng that's the sound or a cry from an animal. A bird, an insect.

Jīmíng the rooster's crow.

A Gǒu is a dog. And a Dào is a robber, a thief or means to steal something

01:08   Jī míng gǒu dào. Rooster Call Dog Thief. Hmmmmm that doesn't make any sense. Looks like we'll be stuck having to know the story behind it.

01:20   Our story today takes place during the time of King Zhāoxiāng of Qín 秦昭襄王 who reigned 307 to 250 BCE. He was the great grandfather of Qín Shǐhuáng, the first emperor in Chinese history. Qín Shǐhuáng will declare himself emperor thirty years after the passing of this King Zhāoxiāng.

01:44   So this story, like so many chengyu's was rooted in the Warring States Period that took place during the second half of the Eastern Zhou. It was a bloody period and underneath the Yellow River valley from Shǎnxī to Shāndōng are buried relics left over from the battlefields of that era.

02:03   The Qín State, if you recall from those China History Podcast episodes 157-158 was, by the time of this King

CHINESE SAYINGS BOOK 1
EPISODE 5

Zhāoxiāng, about to take the fight to the neighboring kingdoms, of which there were six major ones left. So this king was always on the lookout for men of talent that he could entice to come to Qín and become part of what was possibly shaping up to be the winning team.

**02:30** One such man who caught the king's eye was from the state of Qí. Anyone familiar with Shandong province knows Shandong is the land of Qí and Lǔ. Qí Lǔ Liángguó 齐鲁两国. Confucius came from the State of Lǔ.

**02:43** And from the State of Qí came a famous nobleman named Lord Mèngcháng, Mèngcháng Jūn 孟尝君. He was singled out as one of the four most powerful aristocrats of the Warring States Period. So he was rather well-known by all the leaders of all the kingdoms and was a right hand man to the King of Qí.

**03:03** And if you ask anyone already familiar with Mèngcháng Jūn, they'll tell you this guy had a hell of an entourage.

**03:11** Lord Mèngcháng, I guess he couldn't say no to anyone because all you practically had to do was knock on his door and you became one of his clients. These kinds of hangers-on are called Mén Kè in Chinese. Door Guests. So Lord Mèngcháng had a bit of a reputation of being kind, generous and someone who showed up for his friends and anyone else who made it to his ever-expanding inner circle. It's said he had as many as three thousand house guests under his care.

**03:45** And he knew the details of everyone and when it was

# CHINESE SAYINGS BOOK 1
# EPISODE 5

their birthday or their son's mǎnyuè 满月 ceremony, Lord Mèngcháng would be there with a gift.

**03:55** The leaders of the other states west of Qí all wished they had Lord Mèngcháng on their payroll. But nobody wanted him more than King Zhāoxiāng of Qín. He sent an emissary to make an offer to Lord Mèngcháng to come work in Qín.

**04:11** Long story short, he accepted the generous offer and with his whole entire entourage and a load of gifts, he headed west to the Qín capital of Xiányáng. This is near modern-day Xīān.

**04:25** King Zhāoxiāng warmly welcomed him and showed him maximum respect. Lord Mèngcháng presented him with a gorgeous white fox fur coat that just took the breath away from the Qín King. He was astounded by its beauty and softness. But the time being the summer months and all, he told his staff to put it someplace for safekeeping until November-December came around.

**04:51** In no time at all, King Zhāoxiāng promoted Lord Mèngcháng to be his prime minister. And I can tell you the long-serving court officials in Xiányáng didn't like that too much. They weren't happy at all that their king was showing such favoritism to someone who wasn't even from Qín.

**05:09** One of these officials told the King: "How can you trust this guy so much? He used to be the right-hand man to the King of Qí! How do you know he's going to have the

CHINESE SAYINGS BOOK 1
EPISODE 5

best interests of Qín in mind?" Other courtiers as well, worked on King Zhāoxiāng, and after enough lobbying they got him to reconsider.

05:32  But King Zhāoxiāng asked, "What am I supposed to do? He's already here. I invited him. Won't that look bad if fired him suddenly? Look at all these gifts he presented to me! How can I send him back to Qi after all this?"

05:42  His officials told him it's too late for that. He already knows too much. They suggested to kill him. But King Zhāoxiāng, he figured what are the other six kingdoms gonna say when they hear that. So he called for Lord Mèngcháng's house arrest while he tried to think of a solution. So Lord Mèngcháng was kept locked up but he was still well-treated.

06:06  King Zhāoxiāng's brother Lord Jīngyáng had once been a diplomatic hostage of Qí and remembered fondly how well Lord Mèngcháng had treated him. So he went to him and offered his assistance. He kindly told Lord Mèngcháng that his best bet to get out of his situation was to cozy up to Yàn Jī, the king's favorite concubine. She was the only one who could consistently sway the king's mind.

06:34  So Lord Mèngcháng arranged for an exquisite present of white jade to be given to her. But when Lord Jīngyáng handed the gifts to Yàn Jī on behalf of Lord Mèngcháng, she turned her nose up and said if he wanted her help he'd have to get her a white fox fur coat like he gave the king.

# CHINESE SAYINGS BOOK 1
# EPISODE 5

**06:54** Lord Mèngcháng said that was a one-of-a-kind gift and they had to kill a lot of rare white foxes to get it. But Lord Jīngyáng said that was his only way and to satisfy Yàn Jī on getting her to go to bot for Lord Mèngcháng. He had to find that white fox for.

**07:13** One of his entourage told Lord Mèngcháng don't worry sir, I'll disguise myself as a dog and go steal the coat from the gift room. Lord Mèngcháng knew this was undignified but, considering the desperate situation he was in, he okayed the plan. That night, this person disguised himself as a big dog and snuck in through a hole into the room and retrieved the white fox fur coat.

**07:41** It was duly presented to Yàn Jī and, as promised, she pulled through on her end of the bargain, convincing the King at his most vulnerable after a drinking session, to allow Lord Mèngcháng to return to Qí. He agreed and all the permits, papers and documents were arranged for Lord Mèngcháng's safe passage back to Qí.

**08:05** Like Ramses II who came to his senses after freeing the Hebrews, King Zhāoxiāng had second thoughts about letting Lord Mèngcháng go and ordered his soldiers to go bring him back. Just before Lord Mèngcháng passed through Sānménxiá in Hénán, right on the Yellow River, he came to the Hángǔ Pass 函谷关, still there today. And having arrived too late in the evening, he found the city gates closed for the night. Qín rules called for the city gate only to be opened after the roosters let out their first cock-a-doodle-doos.

CHINESE SAYINGS BOOK 1
EPISODE 5

**08:43** Another member of the entourage stepped forward and began doing just that, imitating the rooster's call. He must have been pretty good because all the roosters in the area started doing what came natural. And they were all crowing like crazy. The gatekeeper looked at his watch and said, geez morning already? So he opened the gates and Lord Mèngcháng and his whole entourage passed through safely and at once they made a beeline for Shāndōng Province.

**09:12** By the time the Qín soldiers arrived at the Hángǔ Gate, there was already too great a distance between them and Lord Mèngcháng, so they gave up and turned back. Lord Mèngcháng breathed a sigh of relief and said that on this occasion he escaped from the tiger's mouth by way of Jīmíng Gǒudào. The call of the rooster and a canine thief.

**09:38** And ever since then, someone who resorts to sneaky means of getting something done is described as Jīmíng Gǒudào. People, usually those without much, if any talent, who resort to various kinds of tricks and who cheat to get what they want are also said to be Jīmíng Gǒudào. So, someone who isn't too clever and can't solve problems using their wits and who has to resort to dirty tricks are often described with this chengyu: Jīmíng Gǒudào.

**10:10** So that is our chengyu for this time, about as typical a Chinese chengyu saying as they come.

**10:17** That's gonna be it for this time. As usual, this is Laszlo Montgomery beseeching you to visit Teacup dot media

## CHINESE SAYINGS BOOK 1
## EPISODE 5

if you're so inclined, The China History Podcast, The Tea History Podcast and this Chinese a Sayings Podcast. All available for you. Go check it out. And think about joining me next time, would ya, for another fine episode of The Chinese Sayings Podcast.

Chinese Sayings Book 1
Episode 6

---

# THE HU AND THE HU

狐假虎威—Hú Jiǎ Hǔ Wēi

Back to the Warring States period once again for a story that many of us are all too familiar with.

# TRANSCRIPT

**00:00** Hello again everybody, Laszlo Montgomery here with another pretty halfway decent episode, another chengyu. This one describes a situation most of us working stiffs might have come across at least once in the arc of their career. This chengyu is used to describe people who act big and strike fear in others by living in the shadow of someone powerful. This is the story of the fox and the tiger.

**00:25** And for this one, we have to once again as we so often do, wind the clock back to the Warring States Period, the latter half of the Eastern Zhou Dynasty. So many of these Chinese Sayings seem to come from that era.

**00:40** The source for this chengyu is the Zhànguó Cè, "Strategies of the Warring States," one of the few primary sources of those times.

# CHINESE SAYINGS BOOK 1
# EPISODE 6

**00:50** Today, we're looking at one of the several Warring States, the Kingdom of Chǔ. Mighty Chǔ. No one ever thought this kingdom could be taken down, but they indeed got beat. Our story takes place during the time of King Xuān of Chǔ, Chǔ Xuān Wáng 楚宣王, 369-340 BCE. This is comparable to Alexander the Great in the West, the young Alexander that is.

Today we look at the old classic Hú Jiǎ Hǔ Wēi.

Once again, we break it down uno a uno.

First character Hú, second tone, this means a fox.

The Second character is Jiǎ, in this case means to borrow.

Hú Jiǎ - A fox borrows.

**01:39** Moving right along, we come to another hǔ. But this hǔ, my friends, is not a fox. This hǔ has the third tone, hǔ. Therefore this means tiger. Hú is fox and Hǔ is a tiger.

The fourth character is Wēi. Wēi means power, might, strength, prestige.

**02:00** So Hǔwēi means the might or the power of the tiger.

**02:07** So once again, string it all together, and we get Fox Borrow Tiger Might.

**02:12** Okay, I see some of you nodding thinking you got it. This is like Wheel of Fortune. You perhaps can guess

36

CHINESE SAYINGS BOOK 1
EPISODE 6

the meaning of these four clues right out of the starting gate. Well, like all chengyu there's an ancient story behind this and today's is from more than twenty-three centuries ago.

02:32   Chǔ Xuān Wáng, King Xuān of Chǔ was wondering one day why was it that the people to the north in Hán, Wèi and Qí were so terrified and scared of his general Zhāo Xīxù 昭奚恤. He kept hearing stories about how people particularly feared this one general. So he asked his minister Jiāng Yǐ why was that?

02:57   You had to be careful how you answered these kinds of questions. So Jiāng Yǐ tried to be tactful. He used a fable that he was familiar with to explain to King Xuān of Chǔ. Because it had animals in it, it's a fable rather than a parable. But who am, I to say?

03:14   He began to say to King Xuān that once upon a time there was a fox that wasn't being vigilant and a tiger snuck up on him and snatched him in his jaws. The fox of course begged for his life and said to this tiger it wouldn't be such a wise idea to eat him.

The tiger asked, "Oh yeah, why's that?"

03:36   The fox replied, "You will defy the gods themselves who made me the chief of the forest." When the fox saw the skepticism in the tiger's eyes, he continued, "You should be fearful of their wrath if you dare eat me. Release me and see for yourself how the gods have empowered me and how all creatures of this forest cower in fear and flee at the first sight of me."

**04:00** The tiger thought this over and decided he had better hedge his bets. So he released the fox and followed him closely through the forest to see if his wild claims were true.

**04:12** Sure enough, wherever they went, every mammal, bird, and reptile who saw the fox coming at once began fleeing for their lives. That was quite a scene, the fox walking through the forest, head held high, putting on airs like he actually held this authority passed to him directly by the gods. He strutted and made it look in front of the tiger like they were all running away from him.

**04:40** But you can guess what was going on here. That tiger was giving this fox a full court press and was right on his tail. He didn't want this potential snack getting away. But he just couldn't fail to notice how every animal took one look at that fox and scattered in all directions. Little did this tiger know that all those eyeballs were on him and the reason they were scattering was because of him.

**05:04** The tiger, oblivious to the situation, said to the fox, "You are indeed something else. I can't believe how feared you are in the forest. I guess the gods indeed have made you the chosen one to rule these lands. I therefore must let you go and take my leave."

**05:22** Jiāng Yǐ sighed and said to King Xuān, "You see, General Zhāo Xīxù who is so feared by the people of the north, is the fox. And the king's powerful army that General

CHINESE SAYINGS BOOK 1
EPISODE 6

Zhāo Xīxù commands acts as the tiger. The northern people who flee upon hearing General Zhāo's name, they are the animals in the forest."

05:46 The Chǔ king figured out, it wasn't Zhāo Xīxù the people of the north feared. It was the size and viciousness of his great Chǔ army that was feared. Zhāo Xīxù was only able to act as rough and powerful because he commanded this terrible army with such a fearsome fighting reputation.

06:07 I'm not sure what the English equivalent is. But to bully people by wrapping yourself up in the authority of a powerful backer is what this Chinese Saying is all about. If you're suffering from an abusive manager at the office who's really nothing, but pushes you around cause his brother is the president of the company, that's a clear case of Hú Jiǎ Hǔ Wēi.

06:31 Some secretary or personal assistant who's always giving you a hard time because they work for some big politician or celebrity? Hú Jiǎ Hǔ Wēi.

06:43 Anyone, usually someone small-minded or evil, can be said to be Hú Jiǎ Hǔ Wēi if they use someone else's power to browbeat or force others to put up with all kinds of petty bullying.

06:57 It can even be used geopolitically to describe states who push other states around because they're allied with a greater power.

07:05 Hú Jiǎ Hǔ Wēi. Yeah that's been around since forever.

# CHINESE SAYINGS BOOK 1
# EPISODE 6

**07:11** The fox borrows the tiger's might. I hope this one is indelibly attached to your neurons for future use. If any of you have one of these Hú Jiǎ Hǔ Wēi types in your life, you have my deepest sympathies.

**07:27** Okay, that's it this time. But rest assured I'll be back next week for another useful and interesting chengyu, a Chinese Saying, for your ever-growing collection.

**07:37** Think about wandering over to Teacup dot media to go check out our other China cultural shows, the long-running and internationally award winning China History Podcast and the Tea History Podcast. And much more to come. Just wait and see.

**07:54** And don't forget if you're flying Cathay Pacific Airways, you can also listen to this exact same Chinese Sayings Podcast as well as The China History Podcast. Next to a good night's sleep, nothing helps you beat a fourteen-hour flight more than that.

**08:08** Until the next time, Meine Freunde, this is Laszlo Montgomery wishing you a fond farewell and imploring you to please consider coming back next time for another useful episode, here at the Chinese Sayings Podcast.

**Chinese Sayings Book 1
Episode 7**

## TOO RICH FOR MY BLOOD

曲高和寡—Qǔ Gāo Hè Guǎ

Laszlo digs deep into the Eastern Zhou Dynasty to introduce a Chinese Saying with a story that tells why some music just isn't for everybody.

## TRANSCRIPT

00:00　Hey everyone, Laszlo Montgomery here with the CSP season two opener. I hope everyone had a halfway decent rest while I was busy working on this new slate of ten episodes. For season two I will feature Chinese Sayings that all, in one form or another have something to do with music.

00:22　For example, our four character Chinese saying today Qǔ Gāo Hè Guǎ means the song is too highbrow to be appreciated by many. So before getting more ahead of myself than I already am, let's pick apart these four Chinese characters like we always do and see what this means and what's the backstory behind this unappreciated song.

　　　　Qǔ Gāo Hè Guǎ.

CHINESE SAYINGS BOOK 1
EPISODE 7

00:45   A Qǔ is a song, a kind of sung poetry that became all the rage during the Song Dynasty and even more so in the Yuan dynasty that followed the Song. The four main types of Chinese poetry were Shī, Cí, Fù and this Qǔ form.

Gāo means high or lofty.

01:02   Hè, in the fourth tone, means to join in the singing or to chime in. This character is usually pronounced in the second tone.

01:12   And the fourth character is Guǎ which means few or scant.

01:7   Boy, that was more complicated than usual. So Qǔ Gāo Hè Guǎ all strung together, let's see, poem high joining in few.

01:29   Well, I can sort of maybe make out what this might be all about. But rest assured, like every chengyu there is some ancient story that will explain that oblique four character phrase. And then once you're properly schooled on that, everything will be as clear as a bell.

01:46   Don't roll your eyes or anything but believe it or not, this one goes back to the Warring States Period. Doesn't it always seem that way? 475 to 249 BCE. I'll tell you that was definitely the golden age for chengyu's.

02:00   This comes from a work called Duì Chǔ Wáng Wèn or Replying to the Chu King's Questions.

CHINESE SAYINGS BOOK 1
EPISODE 7

**02:10** And who you might ask who was the one replying to the Chu king? This was someone I'm sure you never heard of. His name was Sòng Yù and he was a literary man of great repute back in the Warring States period. He was an official who was well-known for the profundity of his work and for being a student of a famous official named Qū Yuán. Qū Yuán was a well-known personage from Chinese history and culture. It was from his suicide over his unfair exile from Chu and the later defeat of Chu by Qin that led Qū Yuán to commit suicide by drowning himself in the Mìluó River east of Dongting Lake, which in turn was the inspiration for the whole creation of the Dragon Boat Festival.

**02:57** So Sòng Yù had a very top-rated teacher. This explained why his poetry was so admired by many. And one other noteworthy point about Sòng Yù, he made the list of the Gǔdài Sìdà Měinán, the four most handsome men in Ancient China. So he was a good lookin' guy. Pān Ān, the Western Jin literary great, Gāo Chǎnggōng and Wèi Jiè were the other three. Gao was a general in the Northern Qi and Wèi was another Jin dynasty official.

**03:30** So the king of Chu, after hearing all kinds of trash talking about Sòng Yù around the palace, started to feel a little suspicious about this key man of his. Song Yu had been whispered about and worst of all his literary prowess was put in doubt by many in Chu high society.

**03:50** The King asked Sòng Yù what's up with that? Why is there so much negativity about your work these days? And here in this piece entitled Duì Chǔ Wáng Wèn, like

CHINESE SAYINGS BOOK 1
EPISODE 7

|       | I said, Song Yu defends himself against all these words whispered to the king about him behind his back. |
|-------|---|
| 04:08 | Now, what follows in the narrative from all these Chinese sources is an explanation from Song Yu to the King of Chu that involves all these ancient Chinese musical terms and the notes. So I'm going to try and present it sans the tidal wave of Chinese language terms, which unless you're familiar with ancient Chinese music, will go in one era and out the other. |
| 04:33 | So it went like this. Song Yu began to explain to the king, "Let's say there is a singer performing in the city somewhere. He starts singing some old traditional folk tune from the countryside. Thousands will join in and sing along with him. |
| 04:48 | "Then he performs some dirge or an elegy. Something a little more downtempo and elegant. Suddenly now there are just a few hundred people who can sing along and appreciate it. |
| 04:58 | "Then this singer starts belting out Yáng Chūn Bái Xǔe, an old favorite among the scholarly elites. Now all you have are a couple dozen people who can sing along. |
| 05:09 | "Then when he starts singing all the obscure ancient classic tunes that use all these forgotten keys and high notes and what not, now all you have joining in with the singer are maybe just a few." |
| 05:24 | The king got the message that Song Yu was trying to |

44

CHINESE SAYINGS BOOK 1
EPISODE 7

05:33 — convey. "So the more highbrow the music, the less people will be able to understand and appreciate it."

Song Yu replied to his King, "You got that right. You see, just as the phoenix and the sparrow are both birds, only one can fly to the heavens and back. Can a sparrow ever know how high the sky is? Same with fish. Look at the mighty Kun fish that can swim to the deepest depths of the oceans compared to a common goldfish. Can the goldfish ever imagine how vast and deep are the seven seas?

06:6 — "It's the same with humans. Just as fishes include the mighty Kun and birds have the phoenix, so do people have their extraordinary kinds."

06:20 — The King, after hearing Song Yu carry on like this said, "It must be lonely to have such genius and sagacity," said the King. "You got no idea said Song Yu. You know how it is, Qǔ Gāo Hè Guǎ. If the tunes are too highbrow, few people can sing it. How can the common unwashed masses understand and appreciate my work?"

06:38 — So Qǔ Gāo Hè Guǎ. There are a few different ways as far as how you use it. Like Song Yu, if you feel you're perhaps too ahead of your time or you're just too erudite for your own good and can't get people to follow you, you can resign yourself to the possibility that you are Qǔ Gāo Hè Guǎ. You're too darn highfalutin' for your own good.

07:03 — It can also be used in the situation where, let's say, you're trying to console a friend. Maybe their book bombed or their speech didn't go well or their play got panned. And they were, let's say, under appreciated. Then you can pat your friend on the back and softly, "Hey, Qǔ Gāo Hè Guǎ. Such magnificent work like yours, too clever for these people."

**07:27** Anyone who is recognized for the profoundness of their work yet receives little or no acclaim for it can be said to suffer from Qǔ Gāo Hè Guǎ. Few will sing along to or appreciate a tune that is too highbrow or too intellectual, if you will, for their tastes.

**07:46** There you have it, mes amis. Qǔ Gāo Hè Guǎ. Season Two is now off and running. And that is going to be all I have for you this time. Laszlo Montgomery signing off from the southern California town of Los Angeles. I'm here pretty much each week serving up chengyu, Chinese Sayings, that can be used by your good selves for all sorts of perfect occasions as well as in your daily life, to wow and amaze those orbiting your world. And now you know the story behind this one so if anyone asks you to explain, just remember the King of Chu and the handsome under-appreciated official Song Yu.

**08:30** This podcast as well as the China History Podcast and China Vintage Hour are all available at teacup.media and all the coolest, hippest most respected and admired podcast apps and directories.

**08:43** See you next time perhaps for another exciting episode of the Chinese Sayings Podcast.

# Chinese Sayings Book 1
# Episode 8

## SURROUNDED!

四面楚歌—Sì Miàn Chǔ Gē!

Hopefully, none of us will ever face these circumstances, but when all is lost and you're surrounded by enemies trying to take you down, remember the Songs of the ancient state of Chu.

## TRANSCRIPT

| | |
|---|---|
| 00:00 | Hey everybody welcome back, glad you're still sticking with the program. Laszlo Montgomery here once again with a nice tasty chengyu for you. A special one today. |
| 00:10 | It's special because the story that yielded this particular Chinese Saying is, in my worthless estimation, one of the most famous ones in all of Chinese history. Wow! That's quite a claim. No shortage of well-known stories from the past few thousand years. But this one, it's big. |
| 00:31 | In fact the source from which this chengyu sprang forth is none other than the Shi Ji itself, The Records of the Grand Historian, the part on Xiang Yu, the Xiàng Yǔ Běnjì. |
| 00:44 | This story of the Chu-Han Contention is all rehash from China History Podcast episodes 18 on the Han Dynasty |

# CHINESE SAYINGS BOOK 1
# EPISODE 8

Part 1 and episode 91 covering the life of Xiang Yu. The main characters from both those episodes play a starring role in today's dramatic story behind this Chinese Saying.

**01:08** Today we look at Sì Miàn Chǔ Gē. Four syllables, standard equipment for most all of these Chengyu or Chinese idioms or sayings. And without further delay let's analyze this one.

Sì Miàn Chǔ Gē.

Sì is the number four.

Miàn means your face or to face someone or something, but in this chengyu it means a side of something.

So Sì miàn means four sides.

**01:40** Chǔ means the Chǔ State or Chǔ Kingdom, one of the most powerful Warring States during the Eastern Zhou and again after the fall of the Qin. They were spread out all over Hunan, Hubei and the eastern part of China from Zhejiang up to the southern border of Shandong.

**02:00** And Gē means a song. Chǔ Gē, songs from Chu or Chu folk songs.

**02:07** Combine it all together and you get Four Sides Chu Songs. Ahhh, what can that mean? This is one of those chengyu where the four characters don't give away the hidden meaning. If you don't know the backstory, forget

CHINESE SAYINGS BOOK 1
EPISODE 8

it. You're stabbing in the dark as far as what Four Sides Chu Songs means. So without wasting any more of your precious time with my yapping, let's get right into it.

02:37 You all remember Qin Shihuang, right? The first emperor of China, builder of the magnificent tomb that's the top tourist attraction in Xi'an today, connected all the various walls into the Great Wall. Also a pretty big tourist attraction. Not to diminish his achievement or anything, but he was a cruel tyrant and imposed laws and lifestyles on his subjects that were so draconian and unpleasant that when he died, all these homegrown militias formed and people rose up to get rid of the Qin Dynasty. You all recall from the Rise and Fall of the Qin Part 1 and 2, CHP episodes 157 and 158, the dynasty keeled over and died not four years after the sudden and unexpected death of its illustrious founder.

03:28 Into this enormous power vacuum stepped two giants of their day. One was Xiang Yu of Chu, who I mentioned just before and the other was of course Liu Bang from Han.

03:39 When they were the only two left standing, Xiang Yu and Liu Bang agreed to divide China in half and each would rule their respective kingdom and they'd leave each other alone. This was around August 203. They demarcated China east and west along the Hóng Canal in the middle of Henan. Chu, led by Xiang Yu controlled everything from there to the China coast, as I said, from Shandong to Zhejiang.

49

04:09 | This line separating Han from Chu, all Chinese Xiàngqí or chess players know, is referred to as Chu He Han Jie. Chu River and Han Border, the two opposing sides of the game board, red and black.

04:28 | Well, each king retired to their side of China and word began to soon filter out that Xiang Yu had softened up quite a bit and had become complacent in these peaceful times.

04:2 | Two of Liu Bang's most trusted aides, Zhang Liang and Chen Ping, suggested to Liu Bang that all of China was his if he got rid of Xiang Yu. And now was the time, when Xiang Yu was looking the other way, so to speak.

04:57 | Therefore plans were set in motion to attack Xiang Yu at Péngchéng, which is known today as Xuzhou, fourth largest city in Jiangsu province. The attack was carried out and the final showdown took place in northeast Anhui in the town of Gāixià. Commanding Liu Bang's army was his greatest general Hán Xìn and the Chu army was led by Xiang Yu.

05:23 | Hán Xìn was a brilliant strategist and led Xiang Yu into a number of traps, and after being outmaneuvered and facing one case of bad luck after another, Xiang Yu found himself cornered and outwitted.

05:38 | The panic inside Xiang Yu's camp was considerable and the morale of the Chu soldiers was hitting rock bottom. Food had run out and they were left with no escape route. It was going to be do or die. With Xiang Yu and

CHINESE SAYINGS BOOK 1
EPISODE 8

| | |
|---|---|
| | his army left in a hopeless situation, Han Xin sprung his final trap. |
| 05:59 | He gave an order to all his soldiers as well as captured Chu troops to sing a number of famous songs from the land of Chu. This they did and the sound of all these songs they all used to sing back home in Chu made Xiang Yu's men feel demoralized and pining for their homeland and their families. Whatever will to fight there was, now had left them. |
| 06:26 | Xiang Yu heard this singing too and he wondered if Western Chu had already been conquered and he knew no one was going to come rescue them. |
| 06:35 | And so Xiang Yu rose from his slumber inside his tent and called for some wine. His beloved wife Consort Yú, Yú Jī. performed a sword dance for him and sang to her beloved king and husband one final song, |
| 06:54 | The Han army has conquered our land<br>Surrounded with the Songs of Chu<br>My lord's spirits are low;<br>Why then should I live? |
| 07:05 | And with Xiang Yu's own sword, she killed herself so as not to distract him from what must now be done. And that morning, Xiang Yu, with his last eight hundred troops, fought to the bitter end. All men were lost or committed suicide and Xiang Yu, wounded and at death's door, surrounded by Han troops, ended his own life. He was only thirty years old. |

**07:32** So what this all means, when you use the chengyu Sì Miàn Chǔ Gē, you are expressing being in a hopeless situation beyond your control. If all is totally lost and there's no way out, the forces of nature and fate all lined up against you, you can say Sì Miàn Chǔ Gē. It expresses a sense of hopelessness, loneliness and distressed beyond anything you can control. You're besieged and under attack from all sides, pinned down by your enemies.

**08:06** Sì Miàn Chǔ Gē. It's only used in case of emergency. If you're stuck on the 405 and you're late for a meeting or your financial portfolio took a bit if a hit, you're not in Sì Miàn Chǔ Gē territory my friend. Your world really has to be caving in at least a little for you to be able to say those magic words: Sì Miàn Chǔ Gē.

**08:29** Xiang Yu went down in 202 BCE and Liu Bang of course went on to found the Han Dynasty that lasted all the way till 280 CE. The bedrock of traditional Chinese culture was formed during this fabled dynasty, not to mention a few good chengyu.

**08:47** Again, if you want the longer, more drawn-out, version you can always go listen to those episodes on the Han Dynasty Part 1 and the one on Xiang Yu. Or you can just leave it at this. If you ever saw Chen Kaige's film Farewell My Concubine, it's based on this story of Xiang Yu and Yu Ji, and the Chu-Han Contention, the Chu Han zhi zheng, played out in the background. Sì Miàn Chǔ Gē. Break glass in case of emergency only. The Songs of Chu on all four sides.

CHINESE SAYINGS BOOK 1
EPISODE 8

**09:19** That's all I got for you this time, another musical chengyu for all of you. From Me to You. Laszlo Montgomery signing off from sunny and beautiful LA, the capital of SoCal, Don't forget, the China History Podcast, the China Vintage Hour and this exact same Chinese Sayings Podcast, all available at teacup dot media. And Cathay Pacific too. One more reason to fly them. You can listen to me for fifteen hours. Take care everyone. Come back next time, would ya?

 Chinese Sayings Book 1
Episode 9

## A MAN OF GREAT INABILITY

滥竽充数—Làn Yú Chōng Shù

Everybody knows of someone who can be described by this Chinese Saying. In this week's musical Chinese Saying we look at the lazy poser Mr. Nanguo and his brief career as a Yu player in an all-Yu Orchestra and the wonderful story that gave us a nice useful saying.

## TRANSCRIPT

| | |
|---|---|
| 00:00 | Hey everyone, Laszlo Montgomery here. Okay, I always loved this Chinese Saying. Làn Yú Chōng Shù. It rolls off the tongue quite nicely nicely Johnson. What I particularly dig about this four character idiom is the story behind it. The whole idea about the kind of person this idiom describes just hits the nail on the head. |
| 00:23 | Làn Yú Chōng Shù. Let me dissect it for you without further ado. |
| 00:27 | The first character Làn means to overflow, excessive, and in this chengyu, it means indiscriminate. |
| 00:38 | A Yú is a kind of ancient Chinese woodwind instrument with multiple bamboo pipes all attached together. If you |

# CHINESE SAYINGS BOOK 1
# EPISODE 9

|       |                                                                                                                                                                                                                                                                                  |
|-------|----------------------------------------------------------------------------------------------------------------------------------------------------------------------------------------------------------------------------------------------------------------------------------|
|       | know your classical Chinese musical instruments, it's kind of like a shēng 笙.                                                                                                                                                                                                     |
| 00:50 | And the fourth character is shù which means number or amount.                                                                                                                                                                                                                    |
| 00:55 | And what we're left with is Làn Yú Chōng Shù. Indiscriminate Yú sufficient number. Who in the world knows what that means?                                                                                                                                                        |
| 01:05 | Well, I'll tell you, anyone who knows their Hán Fēizǐ, that's who. This chengyu comes from that great classic of Legalist philosophy. And in the chapter called Nèi chǔ shuō shàng 韩非子·内储说上, Master Hán Fēi gives us today's useful chengyu.                                      |
| 01:20 | Like so many great Chinese Sayings, the story behind this chengyu takes place in the State of Qí. Qí was located where Shandong province is today with its capital at Línzī, present day Zībó. I've been there, but I didn't know it was the capital of Qí when I was there on business. |
| 01:38 | Our royal star of this story is the King of Qí, Qí Xuān Wáng. He reigned 319 to 301 BC. Among other things you could say about King Xuān was that he was a great lover of music. He particularly loved the yú. And King Xuān's royal ensemble, no kidding, had something like three hundred yú players. Yeah, King Xuān liked nothing more than for the entire yú ensemble to play their instruments together as an orchestra at one time. |

CHINESE SAYINGS BOOK 1
EPISODE 9

02:10 | And it wasn't like today with so many freelance musicians having to sing for their supper. These yú musicians got paid well and whenever King Xuān called on them to perform, they got to enjoy a nice meal at the palace and the portions were quite generous. So it was a nice steady, well-paying gig with perks, the dream of many a musician and artist. Not just today. Back then too.

02:35 | And getting top billing in this story was this lovable loser named Mr. Nánguō. Yeah one of those fùxìng 复姓 or two character surnames. Not rare, but you don't meet 'em every day.

02:49 | There were two things Mr. Nánguō enjoyed doing, bumming a free meal off someone and loafing on the job. He was a low-level guy who worked at the palace. In Hong Kong, this woulda been akin to a kind of "A-Sok" kind of worker, like an old handyman or messenger. Somehow he got wind of the sweet deal these musicians had playing the Yú for King Xuān at the royal palace.

03:14 | Looking to get a piece of that action, Mr. Nánguō remembered he actually had this old Yú at his house that had been handed down for generations. So he went and retrieved it from storage, dusted it off and with all those free meals and generous pay beckoning him, he was able to get an audience with the palace musical director who interviewed him and agreed to advocate on his behalf to King Xuān. The king of course said, the more the merrier. So Mr. Nánguō, in no time at all, sat with all the other three hundred Yú musicians and for several years played in the orchestra.

CHINESE SAYINGS BOOK 1
EPISODE 9

03:54   The only thing was that Mr. Nánguō had no idea how to play the Yú. Never took a lesson in his life. He'd just go through the motions and sway with the other musicians and pretend like he was blowing his instrument and totally getting into it. He was one single musician amidst an ensemble of three hundred. No one could tell that he was just going through the motions and not actually doing anything. Three hundred musicians all blowing into their yú at once? if one of them didn't have any sound coming out of it, who's gonna know?

04:29   Well after several years of living off the fat of the land, Mr. Nánguō's gig came to an ignoble end. One day, in 301 BC his luck ran out when King Xuān died. His son became the new king of Qí. This was the infamous King Mǐn. Qí Mǐn Wáng 齐湣王, a king so bad he brought down the whole State of Qí. But that's another story.

04:55   King Mǐn, he liked music too. And when his ministers arranged a little impromptu performance for the new king, all three hundred players of this All-Yú Orchestra started playing. But moments into their performance, King Mǐn shook his head and said, "That's not what I wanna hear. I much prefer soloists. Let me hear a yú recital with just one single musician at a time.

05:21   Mr. Nánguō heard this and his heart started pounding. And he knew this gravy train was leaving the station and he had to get off. So as the king selected members of the Orchestra to each perform a solo, Mr. Nánguō slipped out the back door and exited the music business.

CHINESE SAYINGS BOOK 1
EPISODE 9

05:41 | So this Mr. Nánguō, he was a làn yú, a Yú player indiscriminately chosen for no particular reason other than he owned his own instrument. And he was selected to chōng shù, to make up the necessary number required.

05:56 | So anyone who obviously has no talent but joins the team, and poses as a somebody of talent but was actually chosen cause you just needed a right fielder, they're Làn Yú Chōng Shù. You'd say this in a mocking derisive kind of way. When you say someone is pulling a Làn Yú Chōng Shù, they're someone with little or no talent but they were allowed to join the band or the team just to fill up the required number of musicians.

06:24 | Làn Yú Chōng Shù. The person could be anyone, not just a musician. People in the office, your general manager, workers who come to fix your appliances or your car, your lawyer, your financial advisor, anyone who isn't half as good as they make themselves out to be, you can call them a Làn Yú Chōng Shù. Nobody special. Just someone used indiscriminately to do something, cause you needed something done.

06:51 | And another thing, this chengyu has a secondary use. And may I humbly admit, I've used it myself once or twice over the years. Let's say you are an expert. You play an instrument like a virtuoso or you're a fabulous public speaker or scientist and people call you out and recognize your outstanding virtues. Well, in a self-deprecating way you can just wave them off and call yourself Làn Yú Chōng Shù...nahhhh!!! I'm just an imposter. So don't forget, you can use it that way as well

# CHINESE SAYINGS BOOK 1
# EPISODE 9

to express humility or modesty.

**07:29** So, there it is. That's the story of King Xuān of Qí, personal friend of Mèngzǐ, I didn't mention. He loved music in more of a quantitative way rather than qualitatively. And his son who brought down the house in 284 BC, the wicked King Mǐn, who, because he only enjoyed listening to yú solos, he brought a quick end to the lazy poser Nánguō xiānshēng, Mr. Nánguō.

**07:57** Làn Yú Chōng Shù. To be selected to play the yú just to make up the required number. No one of talent. If ten orthodox Jews want to go pray and there's only nine of them present. Well, they need one more to chōng shù to make up the required ten to make up the minyon. That tenth Jew, didn't matter if never went to shul or even believed in God. He was a Làn Yú Chōng Shù, someone indiscriminately chosen just to make up the required number.

**08:27** So Làn Yú Chōng Shù, you can say that about yourself. But don't catch anyone else saying that about you.

**08:34** OK, that's all I got for you. Thanks for listening and I do hope you'll consider coming back next time for another exciting episode of the Chinese Sayings Podcast.

 Chinese Sayings Book 1
Episode 10

## TRUE TO HIS WORD

完璧归赵—Wán Bì Guī Zhào

In this episode Sima Xiangru promises his king if the precious He Shi Bi jade ornament should get stolen or lost, he will find it and return it safely to his home state of Zhao all in one piece.

## TRANSCRIPT

| | |
|---|---|
| 00:00 | Hey everyone, Laszlo Montgomery back again with the Chinese Sayings Podcast Season 3 opener. I have ten nice chéngyǔ's all lined up for you and the theme for this season will be Soldiers and Heroes. Every episode will feature a chéngyǔ starring a military person or someone who exhibited heroic tendencies. |
| 00:23 | Today is the first of a two-part miniseries that features Chinese Sayings that came from one respected Warring States hero. He was from the State of Zhào and his name was named Lìn Xiāngrú. That's fourth tone Lìn, not the usual shuāngmù Lín 林. |
| 00:42 | So from Lìn Xiāngrú we're getting not one, but two famous and memorable chéngyǔ. And today we look at the one that came first. This was Wán Bì Guī Zhào. |

# CHINESE SAYINGS BOOK 1
# EPISODE 10

**00:55** — Just like almost all of our featured Sayings in Season 1 and 2, this chéngyǔ has four characters as usual. Let's break them apart.

Wán, the first character, means finish or complete.

**01:09** — Second character Bì. Maybe you've seen these before. A bì is a flat jade disc that has a hole in the middle. In the old days, it was an object used in rituals and ceremonies. These days, they're a Chinatown gift shop stalwart.

Wán Bì, the complete Bì, the complete jade.

**01:31** — Guī means to give back or return something. And Zhào, well this refers to the Warring Kingdom of Zhào, also a common Chinese surname. Present-day Zhào state would be spread over the provinces of Héběi, Shānxi, Shǎnxi and Inner Mongolia. Ground Zero Ancient China. Guī Zhào, return to Zhào.

**01:55** — We string our four characters together. Wán Bì Guī Zhào and we have: complete Jade return to Zhào. If you're familiar with the following story, then this all makes sense to you. If not, sit right back and you'll hear a tale, a tale of a fateful trip.

**02:13** — So as I was saying, Lìn Xiāngrú was this model court official who was upright and served his King, King Huìwén of Zhào, to his utmost ability. Rather than always trying to find ways to line his pockets. He always kept the best interests of the state as his top priority.

CHINESE SAYINGS BOOK 1
EPISODE 10

02:34 | As Sīmǎ Qiān wrote in the Records of the Grand Historian, the Shǐ Jì, under King Huìwén, Zhào's fortunes peaked. But they had a badass next-door neighbor who had grand designs on them not to mention the other five states leftover from the Zhōu Dynasty. This predator of course was the Kingdom of Qín, led by the Yíng clan. And their current ruler Zhāoxiāng, building on all the reforms previous to his reign, had completely transformed Qín into a fighting force that had quickly earned a reputation for their discipline and viciousness on the battlefield. And as I said, King Zhāoxiāng was looking for a few good acquisitions.

03:19 | As our story goes, one day back in Hándān, the capital of Zhào, King Huìwén received a diplomat from Qín who had an offer from King Zhāoxiāng. The Qín King in the missive, said that he had heard it through the grapevine that the famous Hé Shì Bì, this fabled jade bì ornament, had somehow come into the possession of the Zhào king. Zhāoxiāng was about midway through a fifty-seven year reign and he was one of those rulers who, when he wanted something, he wanted it now. No excuses.

03:57 | This piece of jade had quite a provenance to it and was even mentioned in the Hán Fēizǐ, the classic eponymous work that forms the central nervous system of Legalist thought. So in 283 BCE, Zhaoxiang told his messenger to go to Hándān and promise King Huiwen that in exchange for this Jade Bì, he was offering fifteen cities inside Qín that he would hand over to Zhào.

CHINESE SAYINGS BOOK 1
EPISODE 10

04:26 | That wasn't a small prize. You could tax farm those places and make a hefty sum, not to mention conscript soldiers and laborers. Fifteen cities.

04:36 | The Zhào King Huìwén called his most trusted advisor, Lìn Xiāngrú and instructed him to take the He Shi Bi to the Qin capital at Xiányáng near modern day Xīān, and hand over the Bì for these fifteen cities.

04:53 | Lìn Xiāngrú was a little bit smarter than his sovereign and he knew King Zhāoxiāng of Qín was a man who famously couldn't be trusted. So Lìn was wary about this offer as well as this mission. But the order came from his king so he had no choice in the matter. Just the same, he decided to show extra caution in handing over the Jade.

05:17 | Lìn Xiāngrú thereupon started headed west in the direction of Qín. The Hé Shì Bì was with him at all times. He had promised his king that he would carry out this job for him and if the Qín ruler reneged on his side of the bargain, he'd return the Hé Shì Bì to Zhao, all in one piece.

05:37 | He arrived in Xianyang and Lìn Xiāngrú, on behalf of the King of Zhào, ceremoniously handed over the jade to King Zhāoxiāng. And then Lìn Xiāngrú retired to his suite of rooms to wait for the deeds and documents to be handed over giving Zhào title to these promised fifteen cities.

05:58 | To make a long story short, Lìn Xiāngrú wasn't far from

CHINESE SAYINGS BOOK 1
EPISODE 10

the mark with respect to what followed. He called that one right. He waited and waited and waited and of course King Zhāoxiāng, DK'd him, he didn't know who he was when Lìn Xiāngrú started pressing the king to honor his side of the deal. So now all was out in the open, King Zhāoxiāng was telling Lìn Xiāngrú and therefore the state of Zhào, thanks for the Hé Shì Bì. I decided not to hand over the fifteen cities.

06:30　So Lìn Xiāngrú was in a bit of a bind. King Zhāoxiāng had the Hé Shì Bì and the fifteen states. Lìn Xiāngrú couldn't go back to Zhao empty-handed, especially not after making such a solemn promise to his King. So he came up with a plan.

06:46　He spread the word around that the Hé Shì Bì had a flaw in it that greatly diminished its value as a ritual or ceremonial object. One of the Qin king's men ran back and told him this and Zhāoxiāng was up in arms. What flaw? What was wrong with it? No one ever said anything like this before? So with Hé Shì Bì in hand, the king summoned Lìn Xiāngrú to the palace and demanded to know what's up with that.

07:14　Lìn Xiāngrú took the Hé Shì Bì from King Zhāoxiāng and jumped back and raised it above his head and threatened to smash it to pieces on the ground if anyone tried to molest him. And he furthermore said he would smash his head against one of the pillars in the palace and bash his own brains out. This threw the palace into an uproar. You didn't see something like this every day. Lìn Xiāngrú at last demanded the king wait three days,

CHINESE SAYINGS BOOK 1
EPISODE 10

fast and reflect on this matter, or else.

07:46 Everyone retired to their sides and for the next few days things settled down. This was 283 BCE. No one knew yet that in sixty-years the Qín would defeat all the warring states and unify China and start an empire. And Lìn Xiāngrú was a diplomat from Zhao and causing him any harm or coming under suspicion for a diplomat's death was a major headache back in the Eastern Zhou days. So most monarch's wanted to avoid getting caught up in these kind of diplomatic uproars.

08:19 Before meeting again with King Zhāoxiāng. Lìn Xiāngrú passed the Hé Shì Bì to one of his underlings and instructed him to head back to Handan, 750 kilometers away, post haste. The trusty aide took off at once and did just as instructed, returning to Hándān via Wèinán, Zhèngzhōu and Ānyáng.

08:39 Lìn Xiāngrú, however, he remained behind in Qín to face the music. He had deceived the king of Qín. But didn't King Zhāoxiāng cheat Lìn Xiāngrú by promising the fifteen cities in return for the Hé Shì Bì? What could he do? It was all out in the open. Everyone knew. He couldn't kill him now? What would people say? So with his teeth grinding and seething with anger, the king allowed Lìn Xiāngrú to return home to Zhào.

09:10 Lìn arrived back in Handan and was given a hero's welcome. This was his big moment. He had not only brought back the Hé Shì Bì back to Zhào intact, all in one piece, as promised, he had also stood up to the

CHINESE SAYINGS BOOK 1
EPISODE 10

King of Qín and showed him the Zhào people had some backbone. His political career really took off and in no time at all he was chief minister to the King of Zhào. Not bad.

**09:36** As you can imagine this matter of Wánbì, the complete bi, meaning the Hé Shì Bì, being gūi, returned to Zhào was a big deal back then. Wán Bì Guī Zhào. The whole jade returned to Zhào. When you say you're going to give something back to someone or to return something to its rightful owner, that's a Wán Bì Guī Zhào situation. This chengyu doesn't have that many uses. I can tell you over the last thirty years or so I've found myself in a few situations where I used it myself. Always gets a good laugh...

**10:10** Okay, that's the inside word on Lìn Xiāngrú, Qin Zhāoxiāng Wang and Zhao Huìwén Wang. Next week we'll look at the Sequel to this story. Yes, Lìn Xiāngrú makes an encore appearance. So be looking for that.

**10:25** Until then mes amis, we're off and running, this is Laszlo Montgomery signing off from Los Angeles, California. I'm not going anywhere so do consider coming back next week for another juicy Chinese Saying. It'll be a good one I promise. Take care everyone.

# Chinese Sayings Book 1
# Episode 11

---

## SO SORRY!

负荆请罪—Fù Jīng Qǐng Zuì

We continue on with another story featuring the great statesman from the Warring States period, Lin Xiangru. After becoming a hero last episode for returning the He Shi Bi Jade back to Zhao, Lin rose high in the government. But the mighty general Lian Po wasn't satisfied to play second fiddle and was determined to put Lin Xiangru in his place. He should have known better and learned a great lesson.

## TRANSCRIPT

**00:00** Welcome back ladies and gentlemans to another episode of the Chinese Sayings Podcast. Laszlo Montgomery here, as promised, with more Lìn Xiāngrú. Fù Jīng Qǐng Zuì this time. Another classic from the Warring States Period. 475-221 BCE, or thereabouts. No one ever agrees on that start date. As I mentioned last episode, there were two rather well-known chengyu that are attributed to Lìn Xiāngrú. Last week, we heard the story about how Lìn Xiāngrú returned the whole jade back to Zhao. Wán Bì Guī Zhào.

**00:39** So, let's take a look this time at another classic tale from those good old Zhou Dynasty days. Fù Jīng Qǐng Zuì. Let's break it down to its constituent parts.

# CHINESE SAYINGS BOOK 1
# EPISODE 11

**00:49** First character Fù, to carry something on your back or shoulder or to bear a burden or responsibility, among many other meanings of course.

Jīng, that's a kind of tree but it's short for Jīngjí which means thorns or brambles.

Fùjīng, thorns or brambles carried on the back. Okay, not sure what that means but let's keep going.

Qǐng means to request or to ask.

And zuì means a crime or guilt.

**01:19** Fù Jīng Qǐng Zuì. Carry thorns request crime. Just like last episode, if you're not hip to the stories of Lìn Xiāngrú, I doubt you'll guess what these four syllables add up to.

**01:33** As usual, we have to go back to that great repository of chengyu, the Records of the Grand Historian, the Shǐjì. Sima Qian. In the chapter entitled Lián Pō Lìn Xiāngrú Lièzhuàn, the biography of Lián Pō and Lìn Xiāngrú, there is this story. Like last time, this story also takes place during the time of the pugnacious King Zhāoxiāng of Qin. As I mentioned before, he was a serious warrior-king and under his rule, well the Qin State emerged as the most powerful of the remaining Warring States left over from the Zhou Dynasty.

**02:12** As you recall Lìn Xiāngrú was from the neighboring State of Zhao with its capital at present-day Handan

CHINESE SAYINGS BOOK 1
EPISODE 11

in Hebei. Qin was at this time in the process of taking Zhao down. The two states had been going at it and it's all going to end at Changping in 260 BCE with the destruction of the Zhao army and the victory of Qin. All covered in a previous China History Podcast Episode CHP 157, I believe.

02:42 But that hadn't happened yet and Zhao was still hanging tough. We saw how earlier in 283 BCE Lìn Xiāngrú rescued the precious Hé Shì Bì from the wily and capricious King Zhāoxiāng of Qin. And then we ended last episode with Lìn Xiāngrú cashing in big time on his achievement and he soon found himself elevated to the post of chief minister. This really made Lìn Xiāngrú a major guy in the Zhao government.

03:13 Prior to all this, the most celebrated man in Zhao was the great military leader, Lián Pō. Seeing Lìn Xiāngrú get all this attention was hurtful to Lián Pō's pride. And amongst his closest comrades, when they'd be out drinking and carousing, he'd say he was gonna get that Lìn Xiāngrú if it's the last thing he did. He swore whenever he could, he'd go out of his way to try and make Lìn lose face and he'd try to diminish him whenever he had the opportunity.

03:45 Well, anyone who's been to Disneyland knows it's a small world. And word got back to Lìn Xiāngrú that Lián Pō had planned a long-term protracted war of passive aggression against him.

03:57 And Lián Pō was true to his word. You know, nothing

# CHINESE SAYINGS BOOK 1
# EPISODE 11

big but one after the other, these public incidents would go down. Lián Pō would say something or do something and Lìn Xiāngrú each time swallowed his pride or backed off or said nothing. And people were beginning to wonder, Dang, Lìn Xiāngrú, where's your spine? Not to mention your face? And Lián Pō was feeling good cause people saw how he was showing Lìn Xiāngrú who was the better of the two, despite Lìn Xiāngrú's meteoric rise to the top of the civil government.

**04:35** One day there was this incident at a very narrow road. Lìn Xiāngrú's carriage encountered Lián Pō's carriage coming from the opposite direction. And it was one of those things, one of them had to back up or else they'd be there all day. There were all these ancient and well-worn rules about order and relationship. And according to these traditions Lián Pō, top military guy though he was, was still one rung under Lìn Xiāngrú's ranking on the political pecking order. So Lián Pō should have backed up. But he stood his ground.

**05:11** So Lìn Xiāngrú, senior in rank though he was, gave the order for his driver to back up and let Lián Pō get by. And a lot of people were standing around and of course they saw what happened and people talked, as people do. And one by one, Lìn Xiāngrú's clients and allies began to leave him and his closest friends appealed to him, asking why he was exhibiting so much weakness in the face of Lian Po's blatant disrespect.

**05:42** And Lìn Xiāngrú replied that these matters between himself and Lián Pō were personal and did not concern

CHINESE SAYINGS BOOK 1
EPISODE 11

the state. He continued, Zhao was under an imminent threat from Qin and at this dark hour solidarity needed to be maintained. And so for the sake of keeping peace within Zhao and not causing any political disturbances, he gave Lián Pō a wide berth and didn't make any waves.

06:10   When someone brought this info to Lián Pō, and after he had fulminated about it for a while, Lián Pō privately bowed his head in shame and with a sigh, realized how small and petty he had been, putting his own feelings of pride and self-pity before the welfare of the Zhao state. All along, while he was out and about, thinking what a great man he was, it was Lìn Xiāngrú who was actually the more noble of the two.

06:41   So ashamed of himself was Lián Pō and so filled with remorse was he, that to show his sincerity and demonstrate his deepest humility along with his apology, Lián Pō cut down a bunch of thorny brambles and he tied them all up and strapped the branches to his back. And he proceeded to Lìn Xiāngrú's residence and with every step he walked towards Lìn Xiāngrú's, the thorny branches tied to his back scratched his skin and by the time he arrived at Lin's door his back was a bloody mess. And Lìn Xiāngrú of course got the message and was moved by Lián Pō's sincerity and his unreserved apology and show of contrition. They talked it over and — happy ending — for the rest of their days, these two remained good friends.

07:30   So we can see from this story that the general Lián Pō, he Fù Jīng, carried brambles and thorns on his back and then when he faced Lìn Xiāngrú, he Qǐng Zuì, admitted his guilt or sought a penalty for his crime. He carried these nasty thorny branches on his back, a kind of self-flagellation to show his remorse and then beg for forgiveness from Lìn Xiāngrú.

07:57 So when you really were being a cad or made a big deal about something that you were in the wrong about, this one's for you. Fù Jīng Qǐng Zuì. I'm not saying you should go out and flagellate yourself like Lián Pō, but sometimes, when you really go the extra mile to be a jerk or that other word that starts with A, Remember the deeds of Lian Po who felt he had to go as far as to Fù Jīng Qǐng Zuì in order to make things right.

08:26 Reserved for those times when you need to go beyond the call of duty to show remorse for your actions... Fù Jīng Qǐng Zuì.

08:35 Okay friends and countrymen, that is all there is to say about that one, this time. I hope you enjoyed our little two-part series featuring the hero from the Warring State of Zhao, Mr. Lin Xiangru. Laszlo Montgomery here signing off from scorching hot Los Angeles, California. Consider joining me next time, won't you, pretty much every seven days, for another informative, useful and historic episode of the Chinese Sayings Podcast.

# Chinese Sayings Book 1 Episode 12

## GO FOR BROKE

破釜沉舟—Pò Fǔ Chén Zhōu

For this week's offering, we hear the well-known legend of Xiang Yu, Zhang Han, and Liu Bang. As the Qin Dynasty starts to crumble, Xiang Yu heads to the defense of Zhao State to face off against the ever-victorious Qin general Zhang Han and ultimately the kingship of Guanzhong. Before he engaged Zhang Han in battle, Xiang Yu shouted a four-syllable order to his troops. And we look at these famous words in this episode.

## TRANSCRIPT

00:00 | Hey everyone, welcome back to another informative chengyu here at the Chinese Sayings Podcast. Laszlo Montgomery here with another episode featuring another hero from yesteryear. Today's character getting top billing has already been mentioned in various China History Podcast episodes, and is in fact the featured topic in CHP episode 91. This of course is the great Chu warrior-king Xiàng Yǔ.

00:31 | Today we look at one of the true sacred cows of chengyu. Pò Fǔ Chén Zhōu. These four Chinese characters, like most all of these Chinese Sayings, say a whole lot in only four characters, four syllables. This one has a long story

# CHINESE SAYINGS BOOK 1
## EPISODE 12

attached to it.

Pò Fǔ Chén Zhōu. Let's do the usual.

Pò means to break, to break something.

A Fǔ is a kind of pot that was commonly used in ancient China to make your rice and cook food. Soldiers carried one with them.

Pò Fǔ, to break your cooking pot.

Chén means to sink.

And zhōu is a boat. So chénzhōu, sink a boat.

01:16  Broken cooking pot sink boat. As I intimated just a brief moment ago, this chengyu has a distinguished provenance.

01:25  First of all, it come to us from the most revered ancient source for China history, the Shǐ Jì, Records of the Grand Historian. Sīmǎ Qiān and his papa, Sīmǎ Tán. But the son grabbed all the headlines.

01:40  And the chapter from which this chengyu sprang forth is called the Xiàng Yǔ Běn Jì. And the story behind this sweeping epic concerns the Battle of Jùlù. The Jùlù zhī zhàn. 207 BCE. For Western Civ aficionados, this time period was that of the Second Punic War, the one starring Hannibal.

CHINESE SAYINGS BOOK 1
EPISODE 12

**02:00** 207 BCE—we know what that means in China. The First Emperor Qín Shǐhuáng died in 210 so this was just a few years after his grim passing. And all the intrigue and bloodletting that was discussed in past China History Podcast episodes was in full swing by this time. Qín Èrshì, the founding emperor's son, was now emperor and he was hardly a chip off the old block. He was grossly manipulated by one of the great villains of ancient Chinese history, the eunuch Zhào Gāo. Thanks to this situation, it didn't take long at all for this first imperial dynasty in Chinese history to dramatically and quickly unravel.

**02:45** Qín Shǐhuáng gets a lot of credit for being a great emperor. And rightly so, for a whole bunch of reasons. But everybody breathed a sigh of relief when he died suddenly. Life was harsh and people started rebelling almost at once against the Qín. Some of the pre-Qin Zhōu Dynasty states started to come back to life. One of these was Chǔ. The great and mighty Chǔ state centered mostly around Húběi.

**03:15** As things deteriorated in the Qín capital at Xiányáng, present day Xīān, one of their great generals Zhāng Hán was sent out to put out all these fires with different rebel armies who were spontaneously rising up in revolt.

**03:30** Before the Battle of Jùlù there was the Battle of Dìngtáo. Participating in this battle was a noble named Xiàng Liáng. He was the son of a Chǔ military legend who had gone down fighting against the forces of Qin Shihuang during Chǔ's final days. Xiàng Liáng had a brother who

77

also died. And so according to tradition, Xiàng Liáng adopted his brother's son. And this nephew was named Xiàng Yǔ.

03:57 Xiàng Liáng had started leading Chǔ rebel soldiers against the Qín as soon as word got out that the feared Qín Shihuang was dead. Long story short, Zhāng Hán was sent to put Xiang Liang away and that's exactly what ended up happening at Dìngtáo where the Qin forces, still a force to reckon with, defeated the Chǔ rebel army.

04:21 As soon as Zhāng Hán handed the Chǔ rebels a defeat, he turned on his heels and headed in the direction of the former Zhào state to go deal with an uprising there centered around the old Zhao capital of Hándān. Zhāng Hán laid siege to Hándān. It was looking bad for these Zhao rebels. So their ruler sent word to Chǔ begging for help. The Chǔ leader who had rose up in revolt against the Qin Dynasty, agreed to send two armies to go rescue Zhào from this siege. One army was led by Sòng Yì and the other by a Liú Bāng. Serving as Sòng Yì's deputy was Xiàng Yǔ.

05:02 And the Chǔ King said to Liú Bāng and Sòng Yì, whoever conquers Guānzhōng first, the Qin homeland and part of the heartland of China, would receive the honorific title King of Guānzhōng. Xiàng Yǔ was itchin' to get the show on the road and go attack Qin at Hándān and relieve Zhao. But Sòng Yì first wanted to take care of a little business in Qi, Shandong Province. And he was in no hurry to go relieve Zhao. And then suddenly he

CHINESE SAYINGS BOOK 1
EPISODE 12

started to make a lot of noise about Xiàng Yǔ that was less than complimentary. So Xiàng Yǔ killed Sòng Yì at modern day Tai'an, just south of Jinan. Then he seized command of the army and the next day Xiang Yu and 20,000 rebel troops were Hándān bound, ready to face off against Zhāng Hán.

05:53 End December 208 BCE they crossed the Yellow River. And there Xiàng Yǔ gave the fateful order to his men to prepare just enough food to eat for three days and then smash their cooking pots, Pò Fǔ. And then once this was done they were then ordered to Chén Zhōu, sink their boats.

06:14 There was no going back. They were at the point of no return, crossing the Rubicon. They'd either defeat Qin and rescue Zhào or die trying. And on the battlefields of Jùlù, just to the northwest of Hándān in Héběi province, there were nine engagements. And Chǔ, outnumbered it was said ten to one, fought like Xiàng Yǔ expected them to do, knowing there was no going back. Do or die, baby.

06:42 100,000 of Zhāng Hán's Qin forces were killed and over 200,000 taken captive. And to avenge his uncle Xiàng Liáng's death at Dìngtáo, and also to get out of the hassle of having to deal with feeding and watching after 200,000 prisoners, Xiàng Yǔ had them buried alive. Not sure how he had that taken care of. But it happened at a small place called Yìmǎ south of Hándān, near Sānménxiá. And to this day they are digging skeletons out of the ground that leads many to believe this may have some truth to it.

07:16 | So Xiàng Yǔ had, probably, the biggest day of his life. This was a complete and total come-from-behind victory with the brash young underdog defeating the mighty Qin army under their ever-victorious general Zhāng Hán. Before the battle, Xiàng Yǔ had his men smash their cauldrons, Pò Fǔ, and sink them boats, Chén Zhōu.

07:39 | Remember that one when you go for broke. When you're committed to achieving something and cast your fate to the wind, you're following the example of Xiàng Yǔ at Jùlù. And in the course of world history, Xiàng Yǔ wasn't the only one to adopt this strategy. Alexander the Great after he landed in Persia and Hernan Cortes, Cortes the Killer, when he landed in Mexico and went on to conquer the Aztecs. Both of those conquerors had their own version of Pò Fǔ Chén Zhōu. Damn the torpedoes, full speed ahead. This one will get you all kinds of mileage if you use it sparingly.

08:16 | So despite Xiàng Yǔ having the greatest moment of his career, the other General Liú Bāng beat him to Xiányáng and was able to claim the kingship of Guānzhōng from the Chu ruler. Xiàng Yǔ felt that that honor was rightfully his. Xiàng Yǔ and Liú Bāng from that point on became blood enemies and each was determined to unify China and succeed Qin Shihuang. Those two will go on fighting and contending for control of China. And in 202 BCE the Chǔ-Hàn Contention, as this dramatic struggle is referred to in the history books, came to a dramatic end and Liú Bāng, who like Julius Caesar, Fortune favored so much, emerged as the most powerful force in China. He'll go on to unite the country and his

| | |
|---|---|
| | Hàn Dynasty will get everything organized in China for the next twenty-one hundred years. |
| 09:15 | Xiàng Yǔ will be killed, of course. That's a well-known story that has yielded a few decent TV dramas, movies and Chinese operas. |
| 09:25 | So that is our chengyu for this time. Pò Fǔ Chén Zhōu. Break the pots, sink the ships. Remember that Chinese Saying whenever you too, despite knowing the painful cost of failure, go for all the marbles in achieving your goal. |
| 09:41 | Take care everyone. This is Laszlo Montgomery signing off from the Golden State, somewhere in the city of Los Angeles. I'll be back next week with more chengyu and another story from China's ancient past here at the Chinese Sayings Podcast. |

 Chinese Sayings Book 1
Episode 13

## A MAN OF GREAT AMBITION

鸿鹄之志—Hóng Hú Zhī Zhì

We're in the dying days of the Qin Dynasty with this week's Chinese Saying. The Dazexiang Uprising marked a turning point in the fortunes of the Qin empire. In this episode we meet Chen Sheng, a.k.a. Chen She, whose origins couldn't have been more humble. Hear his story and how he aspired to become the Hong Hu Zhi Zhi concealed away in his heart.

## TRANSCRIPT

| 00:00 | Hey everyone, another week another chéngyǔ. Laszlo Montgomery here. Chinese Sayings Podcast. For a second time in a row, I might add, we're back in the final years of the Qin Dynasty. |
|---|---|
| 00:15 | Today we look at an old saying that many of us with lofty goals and great ambitions might be able to relate to. Hóng Hú Zhī Zhì. This is one of my faves. And a useful one to boot. |
| 00:27 | But before we get into the interesting backstory for Hóng Hú Zhī Zhì, let's put these four characters on the dissecting table and get to know their individual meanings and see if we can figure out what these four |

CHINESE SAYINGS BOOK 1
EPISODE 13

syllables all add up to. Sometimes you can guess the meaning at once. But most of the time, if you don't know the story, you won't be able to decipher the meaning.

Hóng Hú Zhī Zhì.

A hóng is a swan or a goose.

**00:54** Hú also means a swan. In fact, just combine to the two characters into Hónghú and this is the word for a swan. It also has another meaning that comes from the story I'm about to tell. And there are other words for swans too. Hónghú being one of them.

**01:09** Zhī, first tone, once again is a possessive particle that sort of acts as the Chinese version of our English apostrophe. It has other meanings besides that. Won't get into them now.

**01:21** And the last character, Zhì, fourth tone, means will or aspirations, ambitions.

**01:28** Four characters combined: a Swan's ambitions. Hmmm, that could be anything. Anyways, let's see where Hóng Hú Zhī Zhì came from.

**01:38** As I said, this story came from the excruciating last years of the Qín dynasty. Qín Shǐhuáng gone all too soon. Though many would beg to argue, the whole Yíng family of the Qín Emperor going back so many hundreds of years, as soon as they hit the big time and conquered all the remaining Warring States and unified China, they

CHINESE SAYINGS BOOK 1
EPISODE 13

lasted barely a decade and it was over. Last episode, we discussed Pò Fǔ Chén Zhōu, Xiàng Yǔ's bold order to smash the pots and burn the boats and take the fight to the Qin army or bust.

02:13  Today's story precedes all of that Chǔ-Hàn Contention backstory. Today we look at the Dàzéxiāng Uprising and the story of Chén Shèng, and his number two guy Wú Guǎng. Almost any history book will tell you the Dàzéxiāng Uprising was important because that was the first peasant rebellion that erupted following the death of Qín Shǐhuáng in 210 BCE. Following the Dàzéxiāng Uprising others felt emboldened enough to rise up and suddenly there were many rebellions big and small happening everywhere in the Qín Empire. And as I said, it was all over in 202 BCE with Liú Bāng founding the Han Dynasty.

02:58  Dàzéxiāng was just south of Sùzhōu, not the famous Sūzhōu of Jiangsu, the lesser known Sùzhōu of Ānhuì Province. Chén Shèng and Wú Guǎng were a couple of hicks from the farmlands of Hénán who were now minor officers in the Qín Army. Chén Shèng was leading his battalion to an area northwest of Beijing called Mìyún County. If they ever build an 8th or 9th Ring Road it'll pass right through there. Chén Shèng along the way encountered these logistical problems and his troops got stuck in the mud and their march fell way behind schedule.

03:36  Anyways, Chén Shèng knew he wasn't going to make it to the fort on time and the penalty for that was death.

# CHINESE SAYINGS BOOK 1
# EPISODE 13

Remember this is the Qin Dynasty. Legalism. No messing around. If you broke the rules you paid for it. No parole or plea bargaining.

03:52   Rather than face certain death by showing up late, Chén Shèng decided to rebel instead and not only did his troops join in, this wasn't a whole army, less than a thousand men. But so great was the secret hatred of the Qin Dynasty, upon hearing of Chén Shèng's Uprising, many others spontaneously rose up too and they joined his rebel army.

04:17   You see, many many years before Chén Shèng and the Dazexiang Uprising, Chén Shèng was just another Qin Dynasty farmer pulling a plow with his oxen in the fields of Henan. Even though he was just a mere peasant of no consequence, it didn't mean that he was complacent with his lot in life. After a full day of hard work in the fields, dreaming away about his future, Chén Shèng used to tell his pals, "Hey, if any of us ever makes it to the big time, if one of us ever gets rich or attains power, whoever that is must come back and spread the good fortune to the others."

04:35   His friends would all just laugh at him and tell him he was born a peasant and he'd die a peasant and don't have such lofty goals and ambitions. This was the countryside and there was nothing else beyond their village, and certainly not beyond their county, that was of any concern to them.

05:12   Well, no less a man that Sīmǎ Qiān himself in the Shǐ

CHINESE SAYINGS BOOK 1
EPISODE 13

Jì, his masterwork, the Records of the Grand Historian, he re-told this story for posterity and mentioned in the chapter Chén Shèng Shì Jiā that when Chen plowed his fields and listened to the discouragement of his friends, he said the famous words: Yànquè ān zhī hónghú zhī zhì zāi? How can a mere finch understand the great ambitions of a swan? So Chén Shèng expressed his great ambitions this way and scoffed at his fellow villagers whose hopes and dreams didn't go beyond the walls of their small Hénán village.

05:53 Well, July 209 BCE came Chén Shèng's big chance. He was the man with the Hóng Hú Zhī Zhì, the ambitions of a swan. He was thrust upon the national stage.

06:08 Well, his chance came and it went. This revolt that began in the Ānhuvg countryside lasted for six months before it was put down by the Qín general Zhāng Hán. He was the same guy from last episode. If you recall, his unbeatable army ended up getting beaten by Xiàng Yǔ. Chen Sheng wasn't the right kind of leader. As soon as he got a whiff of success it all went to his head and before you knew it he was declaring himself a king and he took his eye off the ball. Zhang Han's forces snuffed this Dàzéxiāng Uprising out by the end of the year and that was that.

06:46 Hóng Hú, a swan. Zhì ambition or will. Hóng Hú Zhī Zhì, the ambitions of a swan. You have great aspirations. So a hónghú is not only a swan, it's also a word that, thanks to this story from the Shǐ Jì, describes someone who wants to go out into the world and do something

CHINESE SAYINGS BOOK 1
EPISODE 13

with their life.

07:08　In any case, that is the absolute skinny on the well-known and well-worn chéngyǔ, Hóng Hú Zhī Zhì. I do hope you enjoyed that. And Hóng Hú, those are two very nice-looking Chinese characters next time you're thinking about your next tattoo and would like to wear your ambition on your sleeve, no pun intended.

07:23　Thanks for listening everyone. This has been my great pleasure. I'll see you next time I hope. I promise to go dig up another good one for you. This is, as always, Laszlo Montgomery signing off from Los Angeles, California. Its sunny and beautiful here. You should come visit. I look forward to seeing you all next time for another useful and thought-provoking Chinese saying here at the Podcast that stays true to its name, the Chinese Sayings Podcast. You know, we had to pay a marketing consultant $75,000 to come up with that name for us. But it was perfect. See ya next time.

 Chinese Sayings Book 1
Episode 14

## HE SURE HAD A LOT OF GALL

卧薪尝胆—Wò Xīn Cháng Dǎn

China History Podcast fans will all know this story from which our Chengyu was derived. This is the early years of the Warring States period. Kings Goujian of Yue State and Fuchai of Wu were slugging it out down in Central China. From this epic struggle between these two neighboring rivals came one of the great stories from ancient Chinese history that has been told and re-told throughout the centuries. Let's hear it one more time in this episode and learn what's up with "lying on brushwood and tasting bile."

## TRANSCRIPT

00:00 | Hello everyone, Laszlo Montgomery here once again with another heroic chengyu for your ever-growing repertoire. I hope after all this time, at least a few of these Chinese Sayings have come in handy at home or at the office.

00:17 | Today's saying concerns a story that was featured in China History Podcast episode 111 on the 6th century BCE Wú State. The Wú capital of course in modern-day Sūzhōu. Way back in the early Zhōu Dynasty they were once a bunch of relative nobodies from a part of China south of the Yángzǐ, considered back in those BCE days to be rather provincial, uncivilized and downright barbaric.

00:48　Our story concerns the rivalry of the two states of Wú and Yuè. Yue was located east of Wu, in and around present-day Shanghai, Northern Zhejiang and parts of Jiangsu.

01:02　So let's get right on it. Today we look at Wò Xīn Cháng Dǎn. Let's break it down and see what's up.

First character wò, this means to lie, as in to lie on something, to lie down.

Xīn means firewood.

Wòxīn, to lie on firewood. Okay.

01:21　Cháng means to taste something, to try some food out. And dǎn means your gall bladder or in this case the bile from the gall bladder, which I am told is pretty bitter, man.

01:33　Cháng dǎn to taste bile. Hmmmmm. Wò Xīn Cháng Dǎn. Lie on firewood taste bile. There's definitely a story behind this one.

01:45　Indeed there is, and as I just indicated this tale is another great moment from ancient Chinese history. The story of Kings Hélú and Fūchāi of Wú and our hero today, King Gōujiàn of Yuè.

CHINESE SAYINGS BOOK 1
EPISODE 14

**02:00** Our story takes place during the two decades beginning in 515 BCE with the start of Hélú's reign in Wú and the later demise of his son and heir Fūchāi in 495.

**02:14** Now where does this all get slotted on the confusing Zhou Dynasty Timeline? Sort of the end of the Spring and Autumn and the beginning of the Warring States. It was a wild time and it lasted centuries. Confucius was alive during this time.

**02:30** Let's talk about Wú. They became a major player in 506 BCE when they, a relative nobody, defeated mighty Chu. The Wu king Hélú's secret weapons as you recall if you heard CHP episode 111 were Wǔ Zǐxū and Sun Wu. Sūn Wǔ of course was immortalized by his book The Art of War, Sunzi Bingfa. Now, with Wu Zixu and Sunzi, the Wu State was shaking things up and the other states were taking notice.

**03:04** But 496 BCE King Hélú died from his wounds fighting the Yuè at the Battle of Zuìlǐ, present day Jiāxīng outside Shanghai. And in his dying breath, he told his son and heir Fūchāi, even though Wú was the aggressor in this case, they had provoked Yue, Hélú implored Fūchāi to avenge his death and seek retribution against the Yuè King Gōujiàn.

**03:34** King Gōujiàn only got to enjoy his victory for a few years. Helü's son Fūchāi, the new King of Wú, was a real aggressive warrior type. He was the Sonny in the family. Like Qin Shihuang more than two centuries later, he had grand designs to unify China with him at the

CHINESE SAYINGS BOOK 1
EPISODE 14

top. Fūchāi had his Wú military beefed up and when he felt ready he went and invaded Yuè. And at Fūjiāo, 494 BCE Gōujiàn suffered a crushing defeat at the hands of Fūchāi's Wu army. And part of the humiliating peace involved King Gōujiàn of Yue serving at the pleasure of the Wu King Fūchāi for three years. Yeah, for three whole years King Gōujiàn had to stoop to the level of a mere servant to Fūchāi. That dutiful son had fulfilled his father King Helǘ's dying wish, to avenge his death and seek retribution against Yue.

04:38 But after three years, Fūchāi let Gōujiàn return to Yuè. That was the deal. And let me say the bitterness and humiliation King Gōujiàn of Yuè had bottled up inside had reached a point of such no return that now it was now his turn to swear revenge.

04:57 So Gōujiàn went back to Yuè and at once began strategizing how to get even. He had had a lot of time to think about this so as soon as he was back in the groove, Gōujiàn hired a couple of capable men to rebuild the Yuè kingdom. At once, all kinds of reforms were implemented and successfully carried out. After suffering that terrible defeat at the hands of Wu at Fūjiāo in 494 BCE, the Yuè State began to come back.

05:28 As for King Gōujiàn himself, he adopted a regimen that was strict beyond all measure. While these political and military reforms were carried out to rejuvenate the state, he led by example, living in a fashion so frugal and bare even the Spartans would have found it harsh. By the way, over in Sparta at the exact time King Gōujiàn was

CHINESE SAYINGS BOOK 1
EPISODE 14

putting himself through this regimen, they were just a decade away from the Battle of Thermopylae. History was going on all over the place.

06:03 Yeah, for ten years Goujian steeled himself and focused only on building up Yuè to the point where he could finally exact his revenge against King Fūchāi of Wú.

06:14 And not only did King Gōujiàn of Yuè test his own endurance and build up Yuè, he also had spies sent to Wu to carry out acts of espionage. Most famous and legendary of these acts was the sending of Xī Shī to Wú. Xī Shī was one of the Four Beauties of Ancient China, the Sì Dà Měi Nü. Fūchāi was a well-known ladies man and when Xī Shī showed up at his palace, the love bug hit Fūchāi at once. He fell hopelessly in love with this tremendous beauty and completely abandoned the important affairs of state, exactly what Gōujiàn of Yuè was counting on.

06:54 You see, Fūchāi, as I said, was intent on making Wú the top power in the divided land that would one day be called China. He got all full of himself and started carrying out wars with all his neighbors. He did one great thing. though. He started digging a canal, the Han Gou that connected the Yángzǐ and the Huai Rivers. His plan was to build a kind of grand canal that would allow him to sail his navy right up into northern China and conquer those states. His canal, the Hán Gōu, was later incorporated into THE Grand Canal that did eventually get built during the Sui Dynasty more than a thousand years later.

**07:39** And not only that, Fūchāi built palaces and monuments to his glory and for his personal pleasure. He built a special one just for himself and Xi Shi to hang at. After a while, that's all he did. He couldn't tear himself away from her.

**07:54** Meanwhile over in Yuè, King Gōujiàn was living a life of extreme personal sacrifice and discipline. It didn't take that many years for King Fūchāi to blow through the whole national wad. He bankrupted Wú with his wars, pleasure palaces, not to mention the Han Canal.

**08:15** As for Gōujiàn, after ten years of sacrificing all personal joys, comforts and pleasures, and after the Yuè civil administration and military had been built up again, he felt ready to exact his revenge. For ten years he had Wò Xīn, slept on sticks of firewood. And Cháng Dan, tasted bile. Yeah, that's right, as part of his regimen he forsook sleeping on a bed and instead just laid out a bunch of branches and slept on that. And he hung a gall bladder, not sure whose it was, from the ceiling of the hovel he lived in. And each day he would taste some of that bile to remind him of his bitterness suffered at the hands of Fūchāi.

**09:03** So in 482 BCE when Fūchāi was off warring with his neighbors, Jìn this time, Gōujiàn led the Yue forces into Wu and killed Fūchāi's crown prince. Fūchāi rushed back and a peace was negotiated. But it was only a temporary peace and in 473 BCE Gōujiàn attacked again and this time there was no peace. Yue defeated Wú. Fūchāi ended up committing suicide and King Gōujiàn had his

CHINESE SAYINGS BOOK 1
EPISODE 14

revenge, for him a dish served up a little cold.

09:39 And after Yuè's defeat of Wu, they themselves fell to Chu, and Chu of course fell to the forces of Qin. So King Goujian of Yuè by Wò Xīn Cháng Dǎn, lying on branches and tasting gall, going through the most painful hardships and sacrifices, made a comeback. And just like he said he would, he exacted his revenge on his tormentor King Fūchāi.

10:03 Again, I invite you to go check out CHP episode 111 on the Wú State... a lot more to this story than what I've explained here. So that's all I have for you this time. Wò Xīn Cháng Dǎn. Sometimes we all have to make bitter sacrifices to achieve some goal or overcome some challenge. I don't mind sleeping on branches, but tasting gall might be taking matters a little too far. But I guess if you want something bad enough, one will do whatever is necessary.

10:33 So, until the next time mes amis, this is Laszlo Montgomery signing off from fantastic LA, as usual. Think about joining me next time, a mere week away, for another exciting and heroic Chinese Sayings Podcast.

 Chinese Sayings Book 1
Episode 15

## GOTTA GET TO THE GYM

髀肉复生—Bì Ròu Fù Shēng

Another classic from the Eastern Han which features the future King of Shu, the great Liu Bei of Three Kingdoms period renown. In this episode, we find Liu Bei catching a breather after suffering a defeat in the service of Yuan Shao at the hands of Cao Cao's forces. During his period of laying low, Liu Bei starts to regret the situation he finds himself in.

## TRANSCRIPT

00:00 | Hey Everyone, back again, Laszlo Montgomery here. Another Chinese Saying for you, a good one if I may say so myself. Anything that comes to us from the Three Kingdoms is good. This one today, however, isn't from the Three Kingdoms period but it does feature Cao Cao and Liú Bèi. Today's story comes to us straight from the dying days of the Eastern Han. It doesn't all officially end for the Liu family until 220 CE, or AD if you prefer.

00:33 | Today we look at another one that's pretty useful, especially when you start hitting middle age. Today we examine Bìroù Fùshēng. Let's pick it apart.

# CHINESE SAYINGS BOOK 1
# EPISODE 15

00:44 | Bì means thigh or your thigh bone. Ròu, we've seen this one before, means meat but in this case muscle or flesh and can also mean flabby. Bìròu, the flesh on the thigh.

Fù by itself means duplicate or reply among other daffynitions. But together with the last character shēng, fùshēng, means to come back to life.

01:12 | Bìroù Fùshēng. Thigh flesh come back to life. Hmmmm. This is one of those that are not terribly self-evident as far as what that means. No choice but to find out the backstory.

01:27 | So as I said, Eastern Han Dynasty, that's where we find ourselves. The Eastern Han, 25 to 220 CE. The capital is in Luoyang but in our story today the capital has moved even more to the east, well just a bit, to the southeast of Luoyang, to the city of Xǔchāng.

01:47 | There was a battle. It ran a few months in late 200 at Guāndù. Two warlords in the north contending for supremacy, Cao Cao on one side and Yuán Shào on the other, with Liu Bei serving on Yuan Shao's side. Cao Cao was stronger and had the young Han emperor under his protection... air quotes around that word protection. This was Yuan Shao's chance to take his power to the next level but alas, Cao Cao out-maneuvered him and once he marginalized Yuan Shao, the north belonged to Chancellor Cao. This was his great moment, the Guāndu zhī zhàn.

02:32 | Well, after Yuan Shao went down in flames at Guandu,

# CHINESE SAYINGS BOOK 1
# EPISODE 15

Liu Bei was in a pickle. He needed someplace to run and cool his heels for a while and lay low following his defeat at the hands of Cao Cao's forces. He sought refuge in ancient Jīng Province. This is mostly present-day Hubei and Hunan. The governor of Jing was named Liú Biǎo. No relation to Liu Bei but they were of the same clan so that counted for something back then. Still does today in some cases.

**03:04** So Liu Biǎo took care of Liu Bei, showed him the utmost respect and accorded him all the rights, privileges and benefits of someone of his stature. He arranged for Liu Bei to be based in Xīnyě just south of Nanyang in Henan Province. And there, Liu Bei stayed for a while.

**03:26** One day Liu Bei and Liu Biao were out together sitting somewhere and discussing affairs of state when Liu Bei excused himself to go to the WC. While he was in the restroom taking care of his business, he randomly touched his thighs and noticed how big and, well, flabby they seemed. He saw how his body seemed to be turning soft on him from all this sitting around in Xīnyě living off of Liu Biao's generosity.

**03:58** When he sat back down with Liu Biao suddenly Liu Bei sighed and then burst into tears, weeping that his bìròu, his thighs, had fùshēng, had come back to life. Well, what he actually meant, as he explained to Liu Biao, was, that all those years past, he had hardly ever left his saddle, fighting in the north and in the south, first against the Yellow Turban rebels, then in the employ of Cao Cao and later against Cao Cao, always on the run.

His body was lean and hard from living this life. Now so many years later he had been idle, just getting fat off the good life Liu Biao was able to provide him as his guest.

**04:45** And worst of all, besides going to flab and being so out of shape, Liu Bei lamented that he had hardly done anything with his life and had no accomplishments to lay claim to. So that's why he was so emotional. As soon as he saw that his bìròu had fùshēng, that's all he needed to see, and he knew right away he had to go do something.

**05:10** Well, Liu Bei does okay for himself. After getting a little too comfortable and popular within Jīng Province, Liu Biao started to get a little uneasy about having him around, so he sent Liu Bei to go engage Cao Cao's generals at what became known as the Battle at Bówàng. And Three Kingdoms lovers will say, the rest is history.

**05:34** So, Bìròu Fùshēng. The future King of Shu Han's thigh meat started to get too soft and flabby. If you feel you let yourself go when once you were lean and mean and as agile as a panther, well, now you know how Liu Bei felt. So Liu Bei really took stock in himself. And this was all the inspiration he needed to get up, get out and get into something new.

**06:00** So, Bìròu Fùshēng. If you feel due to a life of comfort and ease you ended up soft and flabby, do what Liu Bei did and carve out your own place in history.

CHINESE SAYINGS BOOK 1
EPISODE 15

**06:13** So another one to add to your collezione. You have quite an arsenal of chengyu to work with by now.

**06:21** So until the next time this is the same guy as always, the only one willing to accept the meager wages here at Teacup Media. I mean Kam Jie brings me a naicha at 3:00 every afternoon, but that's hardly what I call compensation for the salary they pay me. No health insurance, no 401K matching. Nada. I don't mind. Laszlo Montgomery signing off as usual, from Los Angeles, in an obscure warehouse not too far from Würstkuche. Do consider not making this the last episode you listen to and join me next time for another delightful, and thought-provoking story about some chengyu from ancient times here at the Chinese Sayings Podcast.

**Chinese Sayings Book 1
Episode 16**

---

# THE FOUR-LEGGED SNAKE

画蛇添足—Huà Shé Tiān Zú

Welcome back to the fourth season of the Chinese Sayings Podcast. After three years and seven months, we continue on where we left off with another story behind one of the great Chinese Sayings, or chengyu. This time around we harken back to the "Strategies of the Warring States" to look at the tale of drawing legs on a snake.

# TRANSCRIPT

| | |
|---|---|
| 00:00 | Welcome back everyone, especially all of you who kept bugging me to revive this old show from 2016-2017 that only ran for three seasons, thirty episodes and then pod-faded away on the thin ice of a new day. |
| 00:15 | Well, by popular demand we're back. And to kick the new season off, here is one of the great ones from the Chéngyǔ Pantheon, a mainstay that never fails to make it to the table of contents of any halfway decent Chinese Idioms book, To Draw Legs on a Snake, Huà Shé Tiān Zú. |
| 00:36 | This one has a few good uses and I always recommend to people to keep this one packed away in their utility belt. Because on the street, this one, when used properly |

# CHINESE SAYINGS BOOK 1
# EPISODE 16

really drives the point home.

**00:49** Huà Shé Tiān Zú. Let's look at these four characters. To Huà is to draw. It's also a noun for a drawing, painting or picture. A Shé is a snake. Tiān means to add or increase. And Zú means your foot or leg among other definitions.

**01:11** To draw a snake, add legs. This is one of those Chinese Idioms that you can sort of guess which way it's going.

**01:20** But honestly, not unless you pulled your copy of the Zhànguó Cè, or "Strategies from the Warring States" off your shelf, there's a better than good chance you won't know for sure what's up with these four characters. This book was the famous chronicle of those years during the Eastern Zhou Dynasty when, one by one the remaining warring states all fell victim to each other on the battlefield until there was only one single badass left standing. And that of course was King Yíng Zhèng of Qín who went on to found China's first imperial dynasty in 221 BCE. And in doing so, went down in history as China's first emperor.

**02:03** And the Chūchù 出处 or source of this tale comes from the chapter of the "Strategies from the Warring States" entitled Qí Cè Èr 齐策二. And it sort of goes like this.

**02:13** Down in the State of Chǔ where Húběi and Húnán are both located in our day, there was a master or benefactor of this temple who paid a visit one day to honor and worship his ancestors. And he brought a vessel of wine with him and made an offering to his forefathers up on

CHINESE SAYINGS BOOK 1
EPISODE 16

the alter.

02:32 But after pouring a few cups of wine and after placing them on the alter, there was still a little wine leftover. So there were three guys standing around, temple custodians or guards of sort. And he turned to them, handed the vessel of leftover wine to one of them and said, "Hey, there's still a little remaining. Take it, it's yours." And he walked out of the temple.

02:53 So these three fellas, they're looking at this wine vessel or flagon and they're all thinking the same thing. There's only enough in there for one of them to enjoy.

03:04 So, after all concurring there wasn't enough wine left to share amongst them, one of them says they should hold a contest. And the winner of the competition takes all. They get the wine. So after a moment of consideration, they were all amenable to this proposal. The one who suggested it said, "Let's all see who can draw a snake on the ground here. And the fastest among us who first completes their drawing wins."

03:30 The ground was a kind of sand or dirt or crushed stone, something that you could take a stick and scratch out some simple drawing.

03:38 So they all broke off a small branch from one of the temple trees and together they got ready to commence the race. Fastest one to complete the drawing of the snake on the ground got the wine. Seemed simple enough.

# CHINESE SAYINGS BOOK 1
# EPISODE 16

**03:51** So they declared the start of the race and they all began scratching that ground surface with their sticks and as artistically as possible tried to draw a snake.

**04:02** One of them finished first and rather than declare himself the winner. He saw the other two would-be artists were still hard at work drawing their snakes. Knowing that this contest was in the bag, he grasped the wine flagon in his left hand and with his right hand, he decided to show off a little and add an additional artistic flourish to his already completed drawing...

**04:26** And he continued by drawing legs on his snake. And just as he was starting to draw the fourth leg onto his snake, one of the other two finished his snake drawing. And at once he snatched the wine flagon from the other guy's left hand and gulped down that one single serving of vino.

**04:44** And as he wiped his mouth, he began berating the other guy who seemed shocked at losing. And he asked the guy, who in the heck draws legs on a snake? Snakes don't have legs? What were you thinking? All this man could do was bow his head in defeat, knowing he had fumbled the ball on the one yard line, so to speak.

**05:05** So the moral to the story the point made by the author who wrote this in the Zhànguó Cè, the "Strategies from the Warring States", was that this temple custodian, by continuing to draw on an already seemingly perfect work of art, created something redundant and useless that in a way, took away from the otherwise already

CHINESE SAYINGS BOOK 1
EPISODE 16

05:29 quite sufficient piece of artwork that he had drawn.

This man Huà Shé, drew a snake. And then he Tiān Zú, added legs.

05:36 Perhaps you've recognized this in your life? How something already perfect or at least very good is ruined by someone trying to touch it up or add some extra finishing touch.

05:47 In the process of going beyond the main point some people will inadvertently, in their attempt to sweeten up their work, produce unnecessary extra stuff that ends up diminishing the point. By insisting to add a finishing touch it ends up distracting someone beholding it.

06:07 Whether it's some literary work or a work of art, an architectural design, a costume or lovely ensemble, or even a special meal you cooked up. Sometimes when you or someone Huà Shé Tiān Zú, adds legs to a snake, you did something that afterwards was not only unnecessary or redundant, in the end it completely took away from the main point you tried to make.

06:37 Maybe you've looked at some architectural wonder, some new building in your city, if you live in the city and there's some, whatever, a sign or lighting or some adornment and what was otherwise a beauty to behold, now it had this extra touch that you can't take your eyes off of in a bad way. And you can't appreciate the building in a way you might have had "these legs not been drawn onto this snake."

## CHINESE SAYINGS BOOK 1
## EPISODE 16

**07:04** The intended outcome is diminished to one degree or another.

**07:08** Now, the opposite of this chéngyǔ or Chinese idiom is another famous one. It goes: Huà Lóng Diǎn Jīng 画龙点睛…

**07:15** Someone huà, or draws a lóng, a dragon. And diǎnjīng, adds the pupils to the dragon's eyes. And just by adding this finishing touch they completely bring this artistic endeavor to life as opposed to adding legs to a snake which takes away from what the intended outcome was supposed to be. In the case of Huà Lóng Diǎn Jīng dotting or eye on the dragon turns good into great.

**07:44** In a literary example, this finishing touch ends up being the one crucial point that ties the entire story together.

**07:53** Same thing with music. Those extra notes added at the end.

**08:00** So Huà Shé Tiān Zú or Huà Lóng Diǎn Jīng. Adding legs to a snake or dotting the dragon's eye. Make sure you end up with the latter, not the former. Sometimes leaving well enough alone is the wise choice.

**08:13** Okay, that is gonna be it for this one. There's thousands and thousands more out there that I will sift through for you and present to you next time.

**08:21** Hey if you have any favorites that haven't been covered yet shoot me a line at Laszlo at teacup dot media. If you

CHINESE SAYINGS BOOK 1
EPISODE 16

08:55 | didn't have a pen, just go to my website at teacup dot media and you'll find me. I'll add it to the list.

This here's Laszlo Montgomery signing off from Los Angeles California. I share a recording studio with the China History and Tea History Podcast guy, a humble narrator if I ever saw one. Okay, I don't want to Huà Shé Tiān Zú by yammering on any longer. Come back next time, won't you, for another interesting and useful chéngyǔ here at the Chinese Sayings Podcast.

# Chinese Sayings Book 1
# Episode 17

---

## THAT'S WORTH A LOT

价值连城—Jià Zhí Lián Chéng

Today's CSP offering goes way way back to the time of Ancient Chu State during the 7th century BC. The famous "Hé Shì Bì" 和氏璧 jade ornament once again takes center stage. In this prequel, we see how a poor farmer (He Shi) discovers this priceless jade and makes multiple failed attempts to hand it over to the King of Chu. King Zhaoxiang of Qin reneged on his offer to trade a bunch of cities to Zhao State if they would only bring him this priceless Jade Bi Ornament and Lin Xiangru had to head to Qin to bring the whole jade back to Zhao. If something has immense and immeasurable value, today's Saying is perfect to use: Jiàzhí Liánchéng 价值连城.

## TRANSCRIPT

| | |
|---|---|
| 00:00 | Welcome back mes Amies. Another day, another Chengyu. Laszlo Montgomery here with the prequel to the Chinese saying we featured way back when in the season three opener that featured Lìn Xiāngrú, King Zhāoxiāng of Qín, King Huìwén of Zhào and the riveting story concerning the return of the whole Jade to Zhào. Wán Bì Guī Zhào 完璧归赵. |
| 00:25 | You may recall the valuable Jade Bì ceremonial disk that the pugnacious King Zhāoxiāng 秦昭襄王 of Qín, in 283 BCE, "requested" from King Huìwén of Zhào. |

Quotation marks around that word requested. And in return for such a precious object as the Hé Shì Bì as it was reverently called, the king of Qín offered fifteen cities that he would take off the books of Qin and hand over to Zhào, Qin's neighbor to the east.

**00:58** Well, King Zhāoxiāng, once he had that Hé Shì Bì in his hands, he said, "what fifteen cities?" So this led Lìn Xiāngrú to go to Qín to get the Hé Shì Bì back. And after no small amount of theatrics, Lìn Xiāngrú heroically returned the whole jade to his king in Zhào.

**01:19** So before we go any further, let's break down the four characters in this chéngyǔ.

Jiàzhí Liánchéng.

Jiàzhí means the value of something. Jià meaning price and zhí being value or worth.

Lián. In this case it means to link, join or connect.

And a chéng is a city. So you could translate liánchéng to mean connected cities, cities that are all right next to one another.

**01:47** So, Jiàzhí Liánchéng. The jiàzhí, or the value was worth liánchéng, a bunch of cities all right next to one another.

**01:58** Well, in this story we wind back the clock and find out about this jade and where it came from. This jade bì was called the Héshì bì 和氏璧. A Bì is a kind of ceremonial

# CHINESE SAYINGS BOOK 1
# EPISODE 17

jade disc with a hole in the center, one of the most ancient of all Chinese cultural objects. Goes back more than five thousand years to Liángzhǔ Culture 良渚文化 that was centered around Hángzhōu, Zhejiang Province.

**02:26** The Héshì bì. It has quite a story associated with it. And the chūchù or origin of the story is to be found in the Hán Fēizǐ. Scroll ahead to the chapter entitled Hé Shì and you'll find it. Hé Shì was a small-time farmer during the Spring and Autumn period. This was in the mid 8th century BCE. His name was Biàn Hé 卞和. Once whilst walking through the hills near his home in the state of Chǔ he chanced upon what's known as a Yùpú, a lump of jade still enveloped in a big rock.

**03:02** This simple peasant Biàn Hé estimated the worth of this yùpú to be of fantastic value and to show what kind of a guy Biàn Hé was, he went straight to the Chǔ palace and presented it to King Lì 楚厉王. But the Chǔ king wasn't what you'd call an expert in mineralogy and didn't know his nephrite from jadeite. So he called in one of his men from the jade carving workshop and asked him to give it an appraisal. This jade carver haughtily pronounced the jade as worthless rock and said it wasn't worth anything.

**03:37** The Chǔ king didn't like hearing that and commanded his guards to punish Biàn Hé for his transgression. And to teach his subject not to present any future worthless gifts, he ordered Biàn Hé's left foot be cut off. And after suffering through this punishment this hapless well-meaning peasant farmer hobbled away with his big rock

| | |
|---|---|
| | and went back home. |
| 04:02 | Chǔ King Lì died in 741 BCE and next up on the throne was his younger brother, King Wǔ 楚武王. Biàn Hé thought he might have better luck this time and brought the big rock to the palace and humbly presented it to King Wǔ. But same drill as last time. King Wǔ called in one of his people to cop a gander at the so-called jade and give an estimate as to its worth. |
| 04:27 | For a second time the jade carving expert pronounced it worthless and King Wǔ, very disappointed after being given such high hopes by Biàn Hé, ordered his other foot amputated. And poor old Biàn Hé, now footless, crawled out of the palace and returned home all dejected |
| 04:47 | And in 690 BCE when King Wǔ died, despite what he had done to Biàn Hé, the poor peasant cried for three days and three nights mourning the passing of his king. Word of how distraught Biàn Hé was somehow made it back to the palace to the new Chǔ king Wén 楚文王. |
| 05:06 | He summoned Biàn Hé to the palace. And poor old Biàn Hé hobbled in on crutches with the precious jade that he wished to present to Chǔ King Wén. |
| 05:18 | King Wén was incredulous that despite heaven's will that caused both his feet to be amputated, asked Biàn Hé why he cried thus. And Biàn Hé, with tears in his eyes said to his king, "I'm not crying because of this double amputation. I'm crying because I know it is of great value, but both times I presented it to King Lì and |

King Wǔ, it was dismissed as worthless rock."

05:46  King Wén called his palace jade carver over and commanded him to examine the rock carefully and to cut it open and see the supposed treasure that the poor old peasant claimed was inside.

05:59  And so he did. He took his tools and cut open the rock and sure enough inside was a giant, perfect translucent piece of jade. Just with one look they knew this was of immense value. No one had ever seen anything like this.

06:16  So for poor old Biàn Hé's suffering, and for his deep sincerity trying to present such a valuable gift to the throne, Chǔ King Wen commanded the jade to be carved into a bì, which it was, in short order. And this jade bì was so magnificent and so wondrous to behold. And to honor Biàn Hé he declared this jade object would be called the Hé Shì zhī Bì, The Bì of Mr Hé, which was Biàn Hé's given name.

06:46  And word spread far and wide of this incredible treasure and somewhere along the way, it ended up in the State of Zhào and became very well-known.

06:56  And the Jiàzhí Liánchéng part of it, today's chengyu, well, centuries later during the long reign of King Zhāoxiāng of Qín, 325 to 251 BCE, this warlike tyrant to Qín was well aware of the repute of the Hé Shì zhī bì and to put it mildly, he wanted it for himself.

07:14  So he sent an emissary east to Zhào state, to the capital in

CHINESE SAYINGS BOOK 1
EPISODE 17

modern day Hándān, Héběi province. And the emissary told the the king that the ruler of Qín wanted this bì for himself. And he was willing to offer fifteen cities to Zhào in exchange for this treasure.

07:32  King Huìwén knew with no small degree of certainty that such a request from this particular king of Qín State was tantamount to a demand. And fearing the possible consequences, King Huìwén arranged to have the bì shipped out west to Qín. He didn't know whether or not King Zhāoxiāng was going to pull through on the promised fifteen cities.

07:54  So this is where we get the chéngyǔ of Jiàzhí Liánchéng. The Jiàzhí or value of this jade bì was worth liánchéng, a bunch of cities joined together.

08:07  Accompanying the bì to the Qín capital at Xiányáng, near present day Xīān in Shǎnxī province was one of King Huìwén of Zhào's more capable ministers Lìn Xiāngrú.

08:20  And the outcome of this story can be heard in the Chinese Sayings Podcast Season three opener that tells the story of Lìn Xiāngrú's visit to Qín and his act of returning the Hé Shì Bì to Zhào. And this Jade Bì went from Qín, to Hàn, to Wèi, to Jìn to Suí and Táng, and was a most sacred ceremonial object.

08:48  So that's gonna be it for this episode's Chinese Saying. If you want to express that something has great value, that it's worth a fortune, you can say jiàzhí liánchéng. Its

CHINESE SAYINGS BOOK 1
EPISODE 17

value is worth many cities. Now, I guess it would depend which cities were in the mix, but by any reckoning the value of many cities isn't small.

09:10 | I look forward to seeing you again for more chéngyǔ next time. There's more Chinese Sayings from where this one came from. Take care everyone and let's make it a date for another exciting episode of the Chinese Sayings Podcast.

 Chinese Sayings Book 1
Episode 18

THE TRANSCRIPTS

---

## ONE BAD APPLE

害群之马—Hài Qún Zhī Mǎ

Welcome back to another CSP. This time I'm happy to present to you another great one direct from The Zhuangzi. Everyone's favorite Daoist tells us the story about a young kid from the sticks who had a chance encounter with no less a personage than The Yellow Emperor himself. When engaging the young kid about matters regarding how to rule the world we learn the useful idiom of Hài Qún Zhī Mǎ 害群之马. This one has all kinds of uses and is worth remembering. Enjoy!

## TRANSCRIPT

| | |
|---|---|
| 00:00 | Welcome back everyone. Laszlo Montgomery here with another chéngyǔ, another four-character Chinese idiom that gets the job done when you got something to say but don't have all day to say it. |
| 00:11 | This one I have for you is rather well-known and has a multitude of uses. Hài Qún Zhī Mǎ. Four characters, four syllables, like it is for most of them. But not all. |
| 00:24 | This one, Hài Qún Zhī Mǎ, has one heck of a pedigree. It comes from the great Zhuāngzǐ himself, from his book of the same name, The Zhuāngzǐ. This book along with the Lǎozǐ, are the two most important texts of Daoist |

# CHINESE SAYINGS BOOK 1
# EPISODE 18

philosophy.

**00:41** Let's break the characters down.

To Hài means to harm, to kill, cause trouble.

Qún means a group.

Hài Qún, to harm the group.

Zhī, that's a particle used in place of an objective noun or pronoun.

And a Mǎ is a horse. Zhīmǎ means the horse of the two characters preceding it, the group being harmed.

**01:07** Literally, this is read Harm Group Horse of that group. If you read The Zhuāngzǐ, in the Zá Piān 杂篇, the Miscellaneous Chapters, and are familiar with the story named Xū Wú Guǐ 徐无鬼 you'd be able to figure out the meaning of Hài Qún Zhī Mǎ. But otherwise, you're left guessing. One of those could be anything kind of things.

**01:31** Well, like any excerpt taken from the Zhuāngzǐ, to take it all in you have to sort of turn off your mind, relax and float downstream. So, let's get right on it. 4,700 or so years ago there was a certain tribe that thrived along the Yellow River that was led by a man named Xuān Yuán 轩辕. We know Xuān Yuán better as The Yellow Emperor.

**01:59** One day, the Yellow Emperor and a group of six close friends decided to hop in a cart and go visit the great

CHINESE SAYINGS BOOK 1
EPISODE 18

sage Dà Kuí 大隗 who lived on Jùcí Mountain 具茨山. Not sure where that is, but certainly somewhere in Hénán.

02:14 After following the road that would take them to Dà Kuí's residence more and more, the road fell into disrepair and before you know it, when they reached the wilds of Xiāngchéng 襄城, it became impassable.

02:25 Zhuāngzǐ and his six friends all got out and looked around to see if any local people were around who could offer them assistance with directions.

02:33 After a while, this young kid came along leading a herd of horses.

02:38 The Yellow Emperor greeted him and asked the young'n if he knew the way to Mount Jùcí. The boy nodded his head and said yeah, he knew how to get there. Then the Yellow Emperor asked him what about the great sage Dà Kuí? Any chance you know how to get to his place? The lad nodded again and said he knew where his house was.

02:57 The Yellow Emperor and his friends could hardly believe their good fortune. The Yellow Emperor remarked to the lad how smart he was, knowing not only how to find Mount Jùcí but Dà Kuí's house as well.

03:11 So the Yellow Emperor thought, well, while he had him, he asked the boy, "What about governing the world? Might you know the best way." The kid was hesitant at

CHINESE SAYINGS BOOK 1
EPISODE 18

first, but after being pressed by The Yellow Emperor he said, "Governing the world? Shouldn't be too difficult. It's no different from herding horses like I'm doing."

03:31  He began to explain, "When I was younger, I roamed and played within the six confines of the universe. But later I got sick and my eyesight weakened. A wise old man told me, 'Ride in the carriage of the sun and roam the wilds of Xiāngchéng.' I took him up in his advice and came here. And soon my eyesight began to improve and once again I can roam and play as before, even beyond the six confines of the universe. Therefore I believe governing the world, it's simply a matter of herding horses. It's not that hard to do."

04:08  The Yellow Emperor stood before the young kid and said, "I am the ruler of the world. And in fact how to govern the world is none of your business. But let me ask you while I have you, if you yourself were in my shoes and ruled the world, how would you do it?"

04:26  Once again, the kid was hesitant to respond but after considering the Yellow Emperor's question he replied, "I'd rule the world in the same manner I tend to my herd of horses. I would remove the harmful influences of the herd and then everything will be fine. It's as simple as removing the horse who was a detriment to the whole herd."

04:45  In other words, this young kid said he'd merely apply his work of removing these Hài qún zhī mǎ, these individual horses that harmed the group or the herd, to

CHINESE SAYINGS BOOK 1
EPISODE 18

society at large. And with that, all will be in harmony.

05:02   The Yellow Emperor pondered the simplicity and beauty of the kid's remarks and then proceeded to drop to his knees to kowtow to him. And then he proclaimed the kid his Heavenly Teacher.

05:14   And that's the end of the story. And I can't tell you if the group ever made it to pay their respects to Dà Kuí. But that's not important to the story.

05:23   In English, we would call these Hài Qún Zhī Mǎ's bad apples, black sheep, or bad seeds, people who, by the very vileness or unseemliness of their character, upset everything around them, or ruin things for the whole group.

05:40   So if your workplace has that one person who, because of their failure to perform well or work well with other colleagues, sort of causes the whole operation to run poorly or not as well as it should, they are a Hài Qún Zhī Mǎ. Is there one family relative who lets their problems cause heartache and pain to others? They're a Hài Qún Zhī Mǎ.

06:03   You have to keep what the young man said, whose name was not immortalized by Zhuāngzǐ, and identify that one Hài Qún Zhī Mǎ in your midst and get rid of them. And then all will be cool. Think about that.

06:18   Okay, a quickie for you, short but sweet. The good news is, there's more where this came from.

## CHINESE SAYINGS BOOK 1
## EPISODE 18

**06:34** | Laszlo Montgomery here signing off from Los Angeles, CA wishing you all well and asking you to please keep coming back for more, here at The Chinese Sayings Podcast.

# Chinese Sayings Book 1
# Episode 19

## REJECTED!

虎口余生—Hǔ Kǒu Yú Shēng

Laszlo dredges up another great one from China's ancient times. This one not only features a story from Zhuangzi's Second Book of the Dao (a.k.a. The Zhuangzi) but also stars the great Confucius himself. In this story from the 5th century BC, Confucius is taken on a wild and bumpy ride with the violent and coarse "Robber" Zhi 盗跖. After trying to convince "Robber" Zhi of the error in his ways, Confucius is given a major dressing-down and his philosophy is utterly rejected, leaving The Great Sage with a feeling of Hǔ Kǒu Yú Shēng 虎口余生.

## TRANSCRIPT

00:00 | Hello again everyone, Laszlo Montgomery here with another beauty of a Chinese saying, an epic one, as you can see by the length of this narrative. This one has a multitude of uses and a fine story that goes along with these four characters.

00:16 | If you're familiar with China's mythical past and early Bronze Age dynasties, a lot of these names will sound familiar. A lot of names will get thrown at you in this episode so if you get tripped up, don't fret. Just go to the show notes at the teacup dot media website to find out who these people were.

# CHINESE SAYINGS BOOK 1
# EPISODE 19

**00:38** Once again we have the great Daoist philosopher to thank for this one, good old Zhuāngzǐ, a family favorite of all Daoist leaning people. And it stars Confucius. Yes, Kǒngzǐ or Kǒng Qiū, the most famous person to ever come out of the State of Lǔ in southern Shandong Province.

**01:00** Our chéngyǔ for this time is Hǔ Kǒu Yú Shēng. And without further ado let's break the four characters down.

Hǔ Kǒu Yú Shēng.

A hǔ is a tiger and kǒu is a mouth.

Hǔkǒu, the tiger's mouth.

Yú has a number of meanings, aside from being a common surname, it means beyond or after a certain event but more commonly, remainder or surplus.

And Shēng means to give birth to, to be born, grow, life, unripe and other meanings besides those.

But in this specific example the two characters, Yúshēng means to survive a disaster.

**01:49** String them all together and you get Tiger's Mouth Survive Disaster. I suppose you can guess the meaning but not with any high degree of certainty, unless you know your Zhuāngzǐ.

**02:02** Not only was Zhuāngzǐ one of the greatest Daoist

CHINESE SAYINGS BOOK 1
EPISODE 19

philosophers, second only to Lǎozǐ himself. His most famous book also goes by that name. The Zhuāngzǐ, a.k.a. The Second Book of the Dào. As a work of literature, it's one of the most beloved of all the ancient texts. Though there are plenty of interpretations as far as what this great sage actually meant in his teachings, not to mention the challenges in translating Zhuāngzǐ into a foreign language.

02:35   If you open up your copy of the Zhuāngzǐ to the Zá Piān, The Miscellaneous Chapters, entitled Dào Zhí 盜跖, you'll find today's useful chéngyǔ.

02:47   Besides Confucius, or, his real name Kǒng Qiū 孔丘, this story also features his good friend Liǔ Xiàjì 柳下季 and his bad-ass younger brother named Dào Zhí or Robber Zhí. A Dào is a robber.

03:05   This man, Dào Zhí, Robber Zhí, he had 9,000 followers who he led. And together they terrorized the kingdom of Lǔ, located just south of the Qí State. Qí and Lǔ were the ancient Zhou Dynasty states that made up present day Shandong. Confucius came from Lǔ as well. This Robber Zhí, he and his men wantonly harassed all the various dukes and princes, they dug through walls, broke into houses and terrorized the people, driving away their horses and livestock, kidnapped their wives and daughters and just caused an all around bad vibe in Lǔ.

03:49   Robber Zhí was just about the most un-Confucian person in all the land. Completely ignored the traditional rules of kinship, refused to perform sacrifices and honor his ancestors. He treated everyone just awfully and everyone went to great lengths to avoid ever having to come face to face with him and his gang.

**04:12** One day, Confucius called on his friend Liǔ Xiàjì and said to him, "If one is a parent, one must admonish one's children; if one is an elder sibling, one must educate one's younger siblings. If one does not perform these filial duties, what value remains in the filial bond? You, sir, are a man renowned for his virtue everywhere in the world, yet your younger brother is known as Robber Zhí and he terrorizes the land, and you do nothing to admonish him. In private, I am ashamed on your behalf. I would like to go in your stead to try to convince your brother."

**04:52** To this, Liǔ Xiàjì said, "Confucius, you speak of filial duties and of education. Yet if a child is unwilling to receive admonishments from his parents, or a younger brother to accept the education of his older brother, even if he is naturally quick-witted like yourself, what can he amount to? Especially in the case of my brother Robber Zhí. His mind is as quick as a gushing fountain, and his emotions change as quickly as a hurricane rises; his skill with weapons is enough to fend off any enemy, and his wit is quick enough to conceal any flaw. He will be happy if what you say pleases him, but if you go against his wishes, he will burst into anger and berate you. I beg of you, Confucius, do not visit him."

**05:45** Confucius refused to believe this. And he decided to

CHINESE SAYINGS BOOK 1
EPISODE 19

05:55 school his friend Liǔ Xiàjì and talk some sense into his thuggish younger brother.

So one day he set off with two of his greatest disciples, Yán Huí 颜回 and Zǐgòng 子贡, and together they headed in the direction of Tài Shān, Mount Tài, one of the Sacred Mountains of China, and drove right up to the front door of Robber Zhí's encampment. And as Confucius alighted from his carriage he saw Robber Zhí's men barbecuing chopped human livers and already Confucius was not getting a good feeling about coming here.

06:24 He approached the guard and requested an audience with Robber Zhí. And he announced himself, "I am Confucius of the State of Lǔ. I have heard of the strength and righteousness of your general. Please ask him to grant me an audience."

06:42 When the underlings passed this message to Robber Zhi, he flew into a rage. His eyes burnt like stars, and all his hair stood on end. He said, "Is this not that trickster from the Kingdom of Lu, Kǒng Qiū ?Tell him for me: 'You speak many falsehoods and proclaim that you are continuing the legacy of the Zhou Dynasty Kings Wén and King Wǔ. Your hat is laden like a tree branch, you wear a wide belt of leather, and you spew laughable words all day long. You do not plough, yet you eat good food; you do not spin, yet you wear fine cloth. All you do is wag your tongue all day long, talking of right and wrong and confusing all the kings on earth. All scholars who listen to you become unable to study the laws of nature. Moreover, you falsely propagate the idea of filial piety in order to wrangle official positions or prize money out of the powerful. Your crimes are serious indeed. Get out of my sight, lest I add your liver to my grill!'"

**07:54** Confucius sighed and tried once again for an audience. This time he said to Robber Zhí's man, "I am lucky enough to be friends with Liǔ Xiàjì, and earnestly beg for an audience with your leader." This underling once again brought Confucius' message to Robber Zhí, and Robber Zhí said, "Tell him to come in!" Confucius walked quickly and carefully into Robber Zhí's tent, and kowtowed to him several paces away from where he sat.

**08:26** The sight of Confucius once again stirred Robber Zhí's anger. He stretched out his legs and his hand went to the hilt of his sword, and he roared like a tigress with newborn young: "Confucius, come forth! If what you say is agreeable to me, you may live another day; if not, you've only death to look forward to."

**08:52** Confucius considered this and then he said, "I have heard that there are three earthly virtues. To be born tall, broad, and comely, so that one is pleasant to look upon by everyone, no matter old or young, rich or poor — this is the highest of the virtues. To be so wise that one knows of everything on Earth, and can converse well about all things, is the middle virtue. To be brave, bold, and skilled with weapons, so that one can lead armies, is the lowest virtue. If anyone possesses even one of these virtues, he is qualified to call himself King. And you possess all three. You are eight feet tall, and your

CHINESE SAYINGS BOOK 1
EPISODE 19

face and eyes are bright; your lips are vermilion and your teeth are like precious shells; your voice sounds as clear as a bell. Yet you call yourself Robber Zhí. I am secretly ashamed for you and your ill name. If you heed my advice, I will send ambassadors to the States of Wǔ 吴 and Yuè 越 in the south, Qí 齐 and Lǔ 鲁 in the north, Sòng 宋 and Wèi 卫 in the east, and Jìn 晋 and Qín 秦 in the west. I will delegate people to build hundreds of lǐ of fortifications for you, around towns of hundreds of thousands of people. You would be the lord of all this. You could turn over a new leaf with all the kings you have offended, lay down your weapons and cultivate the land, take in disciples and sacrifice to your ancestors. These would be the actions of a virtuous sage, and this is what everyone wishes for you."

10:32 When Confucius finished speaking, Robber Zhí flew into a rage. "Come on, Confucius! Anyone who is taken in by your talk is a mere common idiot. It is true that I am tall and handsome, and that people love to look at me, but this is a virtue inherited from my parents. Even if you, Kǒng Qiū, did not flatter me to my face, do you think I would not know this? And I have heard that those who shower praise upon you to your face often do exactly the opposite behind your back. Now you tell me of your intentions to position me as ruler over cities and thousands of people. This is bribing me, treating me as any common idiot. Do you really think this is a sustainable course of action? No matter how large a city is, it cannot be larger than the whole world. The venerable ancients Yáo 尧 and Shùn 舜 ruled over the whole world, yet their sons and grandsons haven't got enough land even to stick an axe in. King Tāng 商汤 of Shāng and King Wǔ of Zhōu announced themselves as the sons of Heaven, yet their descendants, too, went extinct. Was this not because they were greedy enough to wish to own the whole world?'

11:48 'Furthermore, I have heard that in ancient times, beasts and birds were plenty and men were few, so people lived in nests in trees to hide from the beasts. In the daytime, they gathered acorns to eat, and at night sought refuge in the trees, and so they were called the Nest People. In those times, they did not know to wear clothes, so they gathered firewood in the summer, and burnt what they gathered in the winter to keep warm, and so they were called Those Who Knew How to Survive. By the time of The Divine Farmer Shén Nóng (神农), what a quiet, free life people led! Their actions were unrestrained; they knew only of their mothers and not of their fathers. They roamed with the deer; they ate what they planted, and wore what they wove. They had no thought of harming others. This was the age of true virtue.

12:44 'But by the time of the Yellow Emperor (黄帝), these virtues were extinct. The Yellow Emperor warred with Chī Yóu (蚩尤) in the wilds of Zhuōlù (涿鹿), so that blood stained the fields for a hundred miles around. When Yáo (尧) and Shùn (舜) were emperors, they designated hundreds of officials. Tāng of Shāng (商汤) exiled his ruler, and King Wǔ of Zhōu (周武王) killed his predecessor King Zhòu of Shāng (商纣王). From those times onwards, the world went by the principle of Might Makes Right. The strong terrorized the weak, and

CHINESE SAYINGS BOOK 1
EPISODE 19

the majority oppressed the minority. Since King Tāng of Shāng and Zhōu King Wǔ, there has been no true Virtue, only disorder and confusion.

**13:31** 'Today, you study the methods by which King Wǔ and his father King Wén (文王) ruled, teaching them to the whole world, with your heart set on passing them down to future generations. You wear the Confucian robe and belt, and your words and ways are false and artificial, but you seduce all the kings on earth with them, for the purpose of enriching yourself and gaining ample rewards.

**13:56** 'You speak of robbers, but there is no robber more villainous than you. Why do they not call you Robber Confucius, though they call me Robber Zhí? You used your silver tongue to hypnotize your disciple Zǐ Lù (子路) into your path. He threw away his warrior's helm and his longsword, and began to follow your teachings. Everyone said you were powerful enough to stop violence and waywardness. But after all, Zǐ Lù made an unsuccessful attempt to murder the King of Wèi (卫王), and was chopped to pieces on the East Gate of Wèi. This failure must be attributed to the failure of your teachings. Don't you call yourself the Scholar or the Sage? And yet you have twice been chased out of Lǔ State, and you have fled to Wèi, found yourself in dire straits in Qí, and been besieged in Chén and Cài. There isn't a safe resting place for you anywhere on Earth. And your disciple Zǐ Lù came to such a sorry end. If the teacher cannot find his place among men, how can one expect his student to become a pillar of society? Where is the use of your set of dogmas?

**15:08** 'No one is more respected than the Yellow Emperor, yet even he could not protect his virtue. He fought on the plains of Zhuōlù in Héběi and spilt blood for hundreds of lǐ. Táng Yáo (唐尧) was not magnanimous. Yú Shùn (虞舜) had no filial piety. Half of Yǔ the Great's (大禹)'s body was paralyzed, and Tāng of Shāng exiled his predecessor. King Wǔ mobilized an army against King Zhòu of Shang, and King Wén was imprisoned at Yǒulǐ (羑里). Everyone respects these six men, but when one examines them carefully, their behaviour is shameful, for they betrayed their own true nature as well as natural laws in search of achievement and profit.

**15:53** 'Bóyí (伯夷) and Shūqí (叔齐) are called virtuous scholars. But they turned down the kingship of Gū Zhú (孤竹国), and starved to death on Mount Shǒuyáng (首阳山). Their bodies were never buried. Bào Jiāo (鲍焦) thought of lofty matters and disdained earthly things, and actually died hugging a tree. Shēn Túdí (申徒狄) had his advice ignored multiple times, and killed himself by strapping a rock onto his back and walking into a river. His corpse was eaten by the fishes. Jiè Zǐtuī (介子推) was most faithful, and offered a piece of meat from his own thigh for Duke Wén of Jìn (晋文公) to eat. But after Duke Wén returned to his homeland, he forgot Jiè Zǐtuī entirely. Jiè Zǐtuī ran away from the city and into the forest out of anger, and was also burnt to death hugging a tree.

**16:43** 'Wěi Shēng (尾生) had arranged a rendezvous with a

CHINESE SAYINGS BOOK 1
EPISODE 19

woman under a bridge, but the woman didn't come. Instead of scrambling away from the rising tide, Wěi Shēng drowned to death while gripping a bridge column. The fates of these six men are no different from a dog torn limb from limb, a pig drowned in the river, or a beggar with nothing but the bowl with which he begs. They were all men who placed too much importance on fame; they neglected their own lives and death came quickly. They did not take care of their own bodies or cherish their natural lives.

17:20 'When people talk of faithful officials, there is no one more faithful than Prince Bǐ Gān (比干) and Wǔ Zǐxū (伍子胥). But Wǔ Zǐxū's corpse was thrown into the river, and Bǐ Gān had his heart cut out. These two people, though they are called faithful officials, are after all laughing-stocks for everyone on earth. From those examples, you can see that even men of Wǔ Zǐxū and Bǐ Gān's caliber are not worth respecting.

17:50 'If you, Kǒng Qiū, had tried to convince me with strange and fantastic tales, I would not have been able to judge their truthfulness. But you have only told me of the real world and its affairs, and I have heard all this before.

18:04 'Now let me tell you a few things about human nature. Human eyes want to see color; our ears to hear sound; our mouths to taste flavor; our essence of life to endure. A man can live a hundred years at most, eighty years on average, and sixty years if he is unlucky. If we subtract from that any time when one is sick, dying, or depressed, we are truly happy only about four or five days a month.

## CHINESE SAYINGS BOOK 1
## EPISODE 19

18:31 | 'The heaven and earth are boundless, but human life is limited. Compare a finite human life with the endless time of heaven and earth: it flies by as quickly as a racehorse passes a crack in the wall. If a person isn't able to live happily and to preserve his own life as well as he can during his time on earth, he is not wise, nor attuned to natural laws.

18:57 | 'Everything you, Kǒng Qiū, speak of as desirable, is precisely what I am trying to avoid. Get out of my sight as quickly as possible, and cease your blabbering. Your set of dogmas goes against human nature, and is deceitful and hypocritical. It is useless to me, as it prevents me from seeking the natural truth. What more is there to say?'

19:23 | Confucius bowed and left the room quickly, and boarded his carriage where his two disciples awaited him. Three times he tried to grasp the reins and they fell from his hands. His eyes were misty and confused, and his face was ashen. He leant his head against the carriage's dashboard, and could not even breathe heavily, for the wind had been thoroughly taken out of his sails.

19:51 | When he reached the East Gate of the Kingdom of Lǔ, he bumped into his friend, Robber Zhí's older brother, Liǔ Xiàjì. Liǔ Xiàjì said, 'I have not seen you for many days Confucius, and I've been worrying about you. You look as if you've been on a journey. I'm afraid you didn't listen to me and went to see Robber Zhi?'

CHINESE SAYINGS BOOK 1
EPISODE 19

20:13 | Confucius gave out a long sigh and replied, 'Yes.'

20:17 | Liǔ Xiàjì said, 'Did he completely reject outright all of your teachings, just as I said he would?'

20:24 | Confucius said, 'That's exactly what happened. My going to see him was as unnecessarily painful as sticking acupuncture needles into oneself when one is not sick. It was as if I had hurried into a tiger's den, played with the tiger's head, and braided his whiskers. How close I was to being eaten alive!'

20:48 | So with that punchline, Confucius summed up the entire experience by saying Hǔkǒu, from the tiger's mouth, meaning Robber Zhí, he yúshēng, survived the disaster to live another day. He narrowly escaped great harm or death and lived on.

21:08 | Hǔ kǒu Yú shēng. When you find yourself in dire circumstances, even life threatening and somehow you manage to survive and live to see another sunrise, you can say Hǔ kǒu yú shēng. You barely got out of there alive, a narrow escape.

21:26 | Well, this one went on a bit longer than your usual run of the mill CSP episode. But considering the chūchù or origin of this idiom comes from The Zhuāngzǐ and features the famous Confucius, I'm sure no one minds this went into extra innings.

21:45 | Okay, that's your Chinese Saying for this time. This is Laszlo Montgomery signing off from Los Angeles in the

# CHINESE SAYINGS BOOK 1
# EPISODE 19

state of Confusion inviting you to come back next time for another educational and informative episode of the Chinese Sayings Podcast.

Chinese Sayings Book 1
Episode 20

## MR. KNOW IT ALL

井底之蛙—Jǐng Dǐ Zhī Wā

Another staple from the "Greatest Chengyu of All-time" Box Set. The Frog at the Bottom of the Well, 井底之蛙 Jǐng Dǐ Zhī Wā. This one has a multitude of uses and comes to us straight from The Zhuangzi. This story concerns a small frog living happily at the bottom of a well. He lived a happy and contented life but remained oblivious to what was going on outside the small space he resided in. He thought he knew everything till Mr. Sea Turtle came along.

## TRANSCRIPT

00:00 | Hi Everyone, Welcome back once again, another day another chéngyǔ. One more sumptuous Chinese Saying for your collezione. Laszlo Montgomery here offering you a quickie of a story behind this staple among Chinese Idioms. I do hope some of you have been putting the ones presented so far to good use. These things are the best.

00:22 | Today we look at the useful Chinese saying of Jǐng Dǐ Zhī Wā. This one has many applications but it's mainly used to describe someone who, you know, talks like they know everything. But actually you can tell, they are pretty much ignorant and uninformed.

# CHINESE SAYINGS BOOK 1
# EPISODE 20

**00:40** It gets broken down this-a-way.

Jǐng Dǐ Zhī Wā.

A Jǐng is a well, you know, where you get your water.

And Dǐ means at the bottom of. Jǐng Dǐ, the bottom of the well.

Zhī, once again, if you consult the Pleco App, which I keep close to my side 24/7, it translates zhī as a particle used between an attribute and the word it modifies. It also means the previous word, in this case Jǐng Dǐ, has possession of the word that follows, in this case, Wā.

Fourth and final character, Wā, means a frog.

So connect the dots and you get Jǐng Dǐ, bottom of the well.

And wā means frog.

**01:24** So that zhī in Jǐng Dǐ Zhī Wā is telling you that frog is at the bottom of that well.

**01:31** A frog at the bottom of the well. That's how the Chinese might describe someone who maybe, their whole life, never left their county perhaps. And would talk about life and all the things that one could possibly discuss. But only from the perspective of their own limited life experience, you know, having never left the place where they were born or grew up. That's all there was to their

CHINESE SAYINGS BOOK 1
EPISODE 20

world. They knew everything. But hadn't been around the block yet, so to speak.

02:00 If you're wondering if there is any story behind this, indeed there is. And it really is one of the pleasures of my life to bring on stage none other than Zhuāngzǐ himself to take a bow for this one.

02:12 It's always kind of a special treat to be able to dip in The Zhuāngzǐ. You never know what kind of fantastical stories you might encounter where animals will converse and people will talk you in circles.

02:25 Zhuāngzǐ wrote in his eponymous work in the Outer Chapters, from the passage titled Qiūshuǐ 秋水 that a frog that lived at the bottom of a well could not imagine what something like the ocean must be like.

02:42 Zhuāngzǐ uses these words to describe someone whose life is so narrow and small, they haven't a clue how big and complex the world is.

02:52 So others who followed would often quote this example of a frog at the bottom of a well to describe someone who talks a lot but is ignorant and small-minded and perhaps even oblivious to the subject they night be yammering on about.

03:07 That's how it all started. But the story attributed to Zhuāngzǐ that wrapped itself around this sentence from the work that bears his name went like this:

# CHINESE SAYINGS BOOK 1
# EPISODE 20

**03:17** There was this frog that lived at the bottom of an old abandoned well. He wasn't a clam but he was as happy as a clam. Down at the bottom of his well he really believed he had it all. What more could there be beyond this perfect little ecosystem he lived in and that he was blessed to enjoy all to himself.

**03:38** One day this big sea turtle was walking near the abandoned well. I guess it must have been near the ocean and he looked down and saw the frog jumping around the bottom of this well.

**03:50** The frog, happy to have a visitor, called out to the turtle and you know, called him brother, and began chatting with him and couldn't help but regale the visiting sea turtle about all the wonderful aspects of his home at the bottom of this well, how perfect it was in every way.

**04:05** The turtle stuck his neck out and peered down inside and a bit of a stench smacked him right in his face and he recoiled into his massive shell. The frog didn't twig on this at all and heartily encouraged the big turtle to come on down and have some fun with him and check out his perfect world.

**04:24** The turtle peered down again at the bottom and contemplated the offer as the frog kept going on about the endless merits of this swell place he had and how good he had it.

**04:38** The frog kept insisting that the tortoise come on down and see for himself. The turtle made an attempt to try

CHINESE SAYINGS BOOK 1
EPISODE 20

but there was no way, with such a giant shell, there was no way possible to fit himself in the well. So he only managed to get a flipper and his head in there before giving up.

04:52　But all the while he patiently continued to listen to the frog drone on about his pad. This frog said: "I can look up anytime during the day and what do I see? Blue sky, my friend. Just look up and there it is. And check this out, a nice muddy floor, perfect for us frogs, plenty of water and food always dropping in. And y'see this? Holes in the sides of the stone wall. Anytime I want to jump inside and rest, just climb inside. Is this not great or what? I got this whole dang place to myself. I don't know what can possibly beat this.

05:31　The turtle looked at this frog at the bottom of the well and thought how small his world must be. He looks up and only sees a small circle of the sky. He jumps around in a puddle of water and thinks that's all the water in the world.

05:47　When the frog finally stopped yapping about life as he saw it, and knew it, living at the bottom of a well, the turtle began to tell the frog all about the Dōng Hǎi, the East Ocean, which was what the Chinese called the Pacific Ocean. He went on to tell the frog how big it was and how you can swim for a thousand miles and it keeps going on forever. And so deep too, like there's no bottom. And no matter the weather, rain or no rain, the water is so plentiful that it always remains at a constant level, that's how vast the ocean was.

# CHINESE SAYINGS BOOK 1
# EPISODE 20

**06:27**    He told the frog that in times of flooding during the period of Dà Yǔ, founder of the Xià Dynasty or the years of drought under King Tāng of the Shāng that followed the Xià and preceded the Zhōu dynasty, floods or droughts, it didn't change a thing. The vastness of the ocean was totally unaffected.

**06:47**    Yeah, the turtle said, looking down upon the frog and his minuscule existence, that may be good for you but for me, I would never give up my life in the vastness of the East Ocean.

**07:00**    The frog, hearing this, as you can imagine was very silent and suddenly realized being a big frog in a small pond so to speak wasn't such a great thing after all compared to what was beyond this tiny little world. Being a Jǐng Dǐ Zhī Wā wasn't as great as he made it all out to be. And he had to be truthful in his admission that he didn't really know that much, never having seen much of the world outside his well.

**07:29**    So, that is the story of the frog at the bottom of the well. He thought he had the whole world figured out and that this entitled him to speak out about how much he knew. But he only had a limited view and was completely ignorant of what lay beyond his little world.

**07:47**    If I had a nickel since 1979 for every time I heard this one used in the wild or used it myself, I'd have enough to get me a Sourdough Jack and a one-piece egg roll at Jack in the Box.

CHINESE SAYINGS BOOK 1
EPISODE 20

**07:57** I suggest keep this one handy in your utility belt for situations where you're trying to find the words to describe people who pontificate about a certain subject but really don't know what in the heck it is that they're talking about. It's got a lot of uses. I've even seen this used to describe politicians or billionaires who get on TV and talk about something that they probably have little or no idea about. You can pull this chéngyǔ out anytime you want to describe anyone who talks a good game but, because of their situation or life experience, sorta has no idea what they're saying.

**08:35** So, once again I'd like to thank the great Zhuāngzǐ for giving us this beauty.

**08:56** Jǐng Dǐ Zhī Wā, the frog at the bottom of the well, ladies and gentlemans

**09:08** And this is Laszlo Montgomery signing off from Los Angeles, at the bottom of my little well. Thanks for listening. Do take care everyone and be my guest next time for another gratifying episode of the Chinese Sayings Podcast.

 Chinese Sayings Book 1
Episode 21

THE TRANSCRIPTS

## MOM OF THE MILLENNIA

孟母三迁—Mèng Mǔ Sān Qiān

The Chengyu, Chinese Saying, for this time is one of the most well-known of all. This story is a staple when discussing the true meaning of a selfless mother who only lives for her children. This is the story of Mengzi's mother or "Mèng Mǔ" and her pursuit of the perfect location to raise her son. It took three tries but after Mèng Mǔ Sān Qiān 孟母三迁, she found the perfect place to raise her pride and joy. Through this, and other demonstrations of doing her best for her son, Mengzi's mother received high marks.

## TRANSCRIPT

00:00 | Hi Everyone, Laszlo Montgomery here. And here's another good one for you, another Chinese Saying coming to you from this podcast show dedicated to the telling of these stories behind many of the great chengyu's gifted to us by the ancients and from China's days of yore.

00:19 | And this one, I dare say, it's gotta be on the top ten most well-known chengyu's of all time. I actually told this story in an old series I did covering the history of Chinese Philosophy when I discussed Mèngzǐ.

CHINESE SAYINGS BOOK 1
EPISODE 21

**00:33** You see, Mèngzǐ, he had a heck of a Tiger Mom, a mother who was selfless when it came to her own well-being. But when it came to her son, there was no sacrifice too great that she'd willingly make to ensure his comfort and protection, and to pave the road for his success in life.

**00:54** Let's look at the four characters quickly and then jump right into the story.

Mèng Mǔ Sān Qiān.

**01:01** Mèng was short for Mèngzǐ, the great philosopher from the state of Zōu 邹国 who did so much for the study and propagation of the thought of Confucius. He said all people were born innately good. Still debating that one. Confucius is known as the Great Sage, but Mèngzǐ is referred to as the Yà Shèng 亚圣 or the Second Sage.

The character Mǔ means a mother. So Mèng Mǔ is a way of saying Mèngzǐ's mother.

Sān means three and qiān means to move. Move one's residence or the location of a business.

**01:40** Mèngzi's mother three move. Not unless you're familiar with this story can you even begin to guess what these characters mean. And its significance.

**01:50** This one goes way back to time of the founding of the Han Dynasty. That's where this story came from. The Western or Former Han to be exact.

CHINESE SAYINGS BOOK 1
EPISODE 21

02:00   It came from a work called the Liè Nǚ Zhuàn 列女传 or The Biographies of Exemplary Women, written by the great Hàn scholar and organizer of the imperial library, Líu Xiàng 刘向.

02:14   Líu Xiàng was a court official in the palace of Emperor Chéng of Han (汉成帝). How this book got written is a story in itself. Whilst serving at the court, he noticed a big change in the emperor ever since he married this dancing girl from his court, Zhào Fēiyàn (赵飞燕). He had made her his Empress. But over time he began to gradually grow colder towards her and slowly lost interest in her altogether.

02:38   To distract herself from her marital troubles, Empress Zhào lived a lifestyle of opulence and luxury, decorating her quarters extravagantly and even inviting a host of beautiful men to entertain her.

02:52   Líu Xiàng, seeing this, grew more and more angry and frustrated at the Empress's behaviour. However, fearing retribution, he didn't dare to raise his concerns directly with the Emperor. His solution was to painstakingly compile a work that became known as the Biography of Exemplary Women, the Liè Nǚ Zhuàn. This work contained stories about the lives of noble and virtuous women. He finished it and presented it to the Emperor.

03:23   He meant this book as a veiled warning to the Emperor about the dangers posed to his court and dynasty by these salacious goings-on in his inner palace. But though the Emperor praised the book and rewarded Liú Xiàng, he never took any concrete action and nothing changed in his court.

**03:42** Despite failing to sway the emperor, the book itself was extremely influential and some of its stories are still famous today, most notably this story of Mèngzǐ's mother.

**03:54** Mèngzǐ was a proponent of 'ruling through mercy', rén zhì 仁治. One of his core beliefs was, as I said, that human beings were inherently good, but that this goodness had to be acted upon and drawn out by education.

**04:09** Education is an important part of Mèngzǐ's philosophy, and one can certainly see why when one considers the extent Mèngzǐ's mother went to to ensure her own son's education.

**04:22** Long ago, when Mèngzǐ was just a child, his father passed away. His mother, Widow Zhǎng (仉), was faithful to her deceased husband and never again remarried. She raised the child alone.

**04:36** The house in which they lived was close to a graveyard. As part of their play, the child Mencius and his friends learnt to imitate the mourners passing by, kneeling, praying, and howling with grief, and pretending that they were hosting funerals.

**04:54** Seeing this behaviour, Mèngzǐ's mother frowned and said, 'This is no place to raise a child.' She immediately moved them to a house next to a bustling marketplace.

CHINESE SAYINGS BOOK 1
EPISODE 21

05:06 | But not long after, the child Mèngzǐ learned to mimic the shopkeepers and merchants, playing at greeting customers and haggling. Seeing this, Mèngzǐ's mother frowned again and said, 'This is no place to raise a child, either.'

05:20 | This time, she found a house near a butcher's. Again, the child Mèngzǐ quickly learnt to imitate the butcher. He would play around pretending to kill sheep and carve meat. Mèngzǐ's mother said again, 'This is another place one shouldn't raise a child!

05:39 | Finally, she found a house next to a school. Every day, scholars went in and out, passing each other politely and bowing ceremoniously the way courtiers did. The child Mèngzǐ saw this and learnt to mimic it as well. Mèngzi's mother was pleased at last, feeling luck at last after her third time moving her residence. Finally she was able to say, 'Here is a good place to raise a child!' And there they settled.

06:07 | And of course Mèng Mǔ's son, her pride and joy, he eventually grew up to become a great sage and philosopher whose words are still studied and acted upon in our modern day.

06:19 | You can use this idiom, Mèng Mǔ Sān Qiān, whenever you want to exclaim what a wonderful mother someone is. Because of their selflessness in raising their children, always showing up for their kids, doing whatever is necessary to ensure they have a good upbringing and are taught the proper rules and etiquette that were critical to a respectable life and career.

| | |
|---|---|
| | CHINESE SAYINGS BOOK 1<br>EPISODE 21 |

06:42 | Those four characters Mèng Mǔ Sān Qiān, they imply that the mother in question, she fiercely protected her children and no sacrifice or inconvenience was too great for her when it came to their well-being and education. She was the living personification of the ideal mother.

07:03 | And with that we're gonna let the curtain fall and bid everyone a fond adieu. I hope you enjoyed this tale, told, I dare say, millions of times since it was first written down in the Hàn Dynasty.

07:24 | Okay, class dismissed. A nice quick one again. This here's Laszlo Montgomery signing off from the town of Los Angeles. And it's one of my deepest hopes that we'll all convene again next time for another exciting episode of the Chinese Sayings Podcast.

## Chinese Sayings Book 1
## Episode 22

# PRODUCED BY THE GODS

神工鬼斧—Shén Gōng Guǐ Fǔ

Another good one from The Zhuangzi, the Second Book of the Dao. This idiom concerns a craftsman in Lu (southern Shandong Province) who was particularly masterful at carving these wooden stands that held ceremonial bells. So great was his workmanship, people who beheld his handiwork declared it was Shén Gōng Guǐ Fǔ 神工鬼斧.

# TRANSCRIPT

00:00 | Welcome back my friends to the show that never ends, Laszlo Montgomery here with another halfway decent Chinese Saying for you.

00:07 | And for the second time in a row, I have another good one for you from the great Daoist philosopher Zhuāngzǐ. As with our friend from last time who lived at the bottom of a well, this one comes to us from the Outer Chapters of Zhuāngzǐ's eponymous book, sometimes referred to as The Second Book of the Dào. And the story behind today's Chinese Saying that I have for you today, comes from a chapter of the book entitled Understanding Life Dá Shēng 达生.

## CHINESE SAYINGS BOOK 1
## EPISODE 22

00:35 | And before I dive right in to the telling of this tale, let's first look at the four characters Shēn Gōng Guǐ Fǔ and break them down into their constituent parts.

A Shén is a god, deity, or some immortal being.

Gōng means a worker or a skill.

Guǐ means a ghost or a spirit.

And Fǔ is an axe or a hatchet.

01:00 | God worker ghost axe. That doesn't reveal too much as far as what the meaning is behind these four characters.

01:08 | Now before I proceed, let me mention this is one of those chengyu that you can turn inside out and say it as Guǐ Fǔ Shén Gōng. Works interchangeably with Shén Gōng Guǐ Fǔ.

01:20 | This one comes to us, no surprise here, from the Warring States Period, the age in which Zhuāngzǐ himself lived.

01:27 | The chapter entitled Dáshēng 达生 contains a series of anecdotes on the theme of 'Understanding Life'. And our chengyu for this episode comes from one of these very anecdotes.

01:40 | The star of this Chinese Saying is named Zǐqìng 梓庆 or Craftsman Qìng or Master Qìng.

01:49 | He resided in present-day Shandong Province,

CHINESE SAYINGS BOOK 1
EPISODE 22

in the State of Lǔ. The reason he was known as Zǐqìng or Craftsman or Master Qìng was because professionally he used to craft wooden stands for ceremonial Chinese bells. These stands were called a Jù 鐻.

02:07　In ancient times music was part and parcel of all the rituals and ceremonies carried out in those Zhou Dynasty days. And these jù, or wooden racks to hold all the different tuned bells, made by Zǐqìng's hands were so delicately carved and intricately crafted that, when people saw them, they exclaimed, 'This must be the work of some god or spirit, not of a man!' Shén Gōng Guǐ Fǔ.

02:36　One day, one of these jù was brought to the royal palace of the King of Lǔ. He was so astonished by its beauty that he summoned Craftsman Qing and asked him straight out, 'By what magical power have you made this?'

02:50　Craftsman Qing replied, 'I am merely an artisan, not a magician. Nonetheless, I have one special skill. Whenever I am about to make a jù, I am very careful to conserve my energy and thought process. Before beginning my work, I fast in order to quiet my mind and calm my thoughts.

03:11　'After three days of fasting, I think no more of whether my work will be famous and celebrated, or what sorts of monetary rewards or grand titles I will receive for my art.

# CHINESE SAYINGS BOOK 1
# EPISODE 22

**03:25** | 'After five days of fasting, I wonder no longer about whether my work will turn out clumsy or elaborate, or what kinds of criticism, good or bad, its viewers will direct at it.

**03:33** | 'After seven days of fasting, my mind disconnects completely from my body: I feel formless, and forget even that I have limbs.

**03:43** | 'This is when I know the time is right to begin my work. With thoughts of the imperial court and outside distractions utterly banished from my mind, I am free to focus on nothing but my craft. In this state, I enter the forest and observe the natural materials all around me. When I find a suitable piece of wood, of about the right shape and size for a jù, I can envision the finished product in my mind. Now all I have to do is take the wood home and add the finishing touches until the jù I envisioned emerges from the piece of wood retrieved from the forest.

**04:21** | 'If at any point this process is disturbed or polluted, I quit immediately. So the Jù that I make always comes from a state of mind that is in perfect harmony with nature. And perhaps for this reason, people see my carving and artistic endeavors and believe them to be supernatural.'

**04:42** | So, using all the modesty of a gentleman craftsman, Zǐqìng explained that it's only because he communes with the forces of nature that people behold his craftsmanship and believe it to be made by the hands of the gods or great spirits.

CHINESE SAYINGS BOOK 1
EPISODE 22

**04:58** You use this idiom to describe something that is so beautifully made that it looks as if it were crafted by supernatural beings. A work of art in a museum, or a mechanical device or anything that is crafted and made in such a way that is astonishing in its detail and perfection. And you can use this term as either a noun or an adjective.

**05:21** You can even ascribe this chéngyǔ to great technological marvels—the Large Hadron Collider, the Webb Telescope, the Tiānwén-1 Mars spacecraft. These two can be Shén Gōng Guǐ Fǔ.

**05:36** Again, you have the option to say this one Guǐ Fǔ Shén Gōng. Both versions of this idiom work all over China. I have it on good authority.

**05:45** So that's all I have for you this time. In and out, just a quickie for you, a versatile Chinese chengyu, gifted to us from Zhuāngzǐ himself, that you can use to exclaim when something you behold, that is made by us humans, appears so incredible and amazing in its construct, you can't believe it was not made by gods.

**06:06** And with that I will leave you for now. This is Laszlo Montgomery once again signing off from lovely Los Angeles, here in the state of California, wishing you well and beseeching you to consider coming back next time for another useful and thought provoking episode of the Chinese Sayings Podcast.

# Chinese Sayings Book 1
# Episode 23

**THE TRANSCRIPTS**

## A HORSE IS A HORSE, OF COURSE, OF COURSE

指鹿为马—Zhǐ Lù Wéi Mǎ

The story behind today's Chinese Saying is an old favorite of all lovers of popular Chinese history. How can we forget Zhao Gao 赵高 from the Qin Dynasty and the famous story behind Zhǐ Lù Wéi Mǎ 指鹿为马. In our connected age when it's so easy to hoodwink one another in news feeds and social media, this is the perfect chéngyǔ to keep handy at all times. And of course, because this Zhǐ Lù Wéi Mǎ strategy worked so well for Zhao Gao in the 3rd Century BC, many an autocrat since, also found it handy and useful, not to mention, effective.

## TRANSCRIPT

00:00 | Welcome back everyone, another day another Chinese Saying. Laszlo Montgomery with you as always. If you're looking for a few nice stories behind some of the more popular and not so well-known Chinese Sayings you've come to the right place.

00:15 | And for our chengyu for this time, I'm featuring a saying that was as true back in the Qín dynasty from whence it came as it is today. In fact, a lot of tyrants from world history pretty much owed their success to the story behind this great Chinese Saying. This one was sometimes the lynchpin on which a few dictators,

CHINESE SAYINGS BOOK 1
EPISODE 23

autocrats, tyrants and authoritarian government leaders owed their position of power.

00:43 China History Podcast listeners all know this one, the story behind these four characters are as famous as the saying itself. Zhǐ Lù Wéi Mǎ. That's right, 207 BC, the final years of the Qín. And we owe this story to none other than el gran historiador himself, Sīmǎ Qiān. And in the chapter entitled Qín Shǐhuáng Běnjì 秦始皇本纪 from this most famous of ancient works of Chinese historiography, the Shǐ Jì, we get this classic.

Zhǐ Lù Wéi Mǎ.

The character zhǐ means to point at.

And a lù, that' a deer.

Zhǐ lù, point to a deer.

Wéi, this is a character with many uses and definitions but for our purposes in this episode it means to act as or serve as or to be or mean.

And the final character, Mǎ, that's a horse.

01:51 Point deer as a horse.

01:56 Not that difficult to figure out, but without already knowing this famous story from 3rd Century BC China, you really can't know for sure, and you certainly can't appreciate it as much.

CHINESE SAYINGS BOOK 1
EPISODE 23

---

**02:08** Top billing in this tale, of course, is none other than the maybe-maybe not eunuch Zhào Gāo 赵高, featured not only in the Qín Dynasty series but also in the Eunuchs of China series, Part 1. Besides the inspiration behind this great chengyu, Zhào Gāo is also remembered as one of the earliest eunuchs and boy, did he ever give them a bad name. He's one of the more reviled personages from Chinese history. So, let's get this show on the road and find out why.

**02:38** No need to rehash the glory years of the Qín Dynasty, nor its illustrious founder, Yíng Zhèng, who reigned as the First Qín Emperor. Let's go straight to the peculiar ending that's a favorite of so many lovers of Chinese history.

**02:53** Whilst traveling out east in between July and August 210 BC near the Hénán Shāndōng border, the emperor died.

**03:03** And that immediately set in motion a concatenation of events that resulted, ultimately, in the fall of the dynasty. After defeating the warring states and founding the Qín dynasty, he only reigned as emperor from 221 to 210 BC, barely eleven years.

**03:22** In a nutshell, with the emperor so suddenly and unexpectedly deceased and still very far from the capital, Zhào Gāo figured why not take advantage of the situation to make a power grab.

**03:36** At that moment in the summer of 210 BC, the First

Emperor's entourage, besides Zhào Gāo, included Qín Shihuang's right hand man and chancellor Lǐ Sī, as well as the emperor's 18th and youngest son, Yíng Húhài 胡亥 who was in his late teens. Even though he wasn't the crown prince, Zhào Gāo came up with a scheme to have the actual crown prince eliminated and then take advantage of the confusion and political chaos following the announcement of the emperor's death to plop Húhài on the throne to reign as The Second Qín Emperor, Qín Èrshì 秦二世.

**04:12** Zhào Gāo knew full well that the emperor wanted the crown prince, Fúsū 扶苏 to take over after he died. But Fúsū was too close to Zhào Gāo's gravest political enemy, the Qín Emperor's loyal general Méng Tián 蒙恬. If Fúsū ended up becoming emperor, Zhào Gāo knew he was finished.

**04:32** On his deathbed, the emperor had written a letter to Fúsū commanding him to immediately return to the capital and be ready to take over as his successor.

**04:42** That letter, of course, was never delivered and as the famous story goes, as told by Sīmǎ Qiān himself, Zhào Gāo conspired with Lǐ Sī to take the emperor's seal, forge a letter to both Méng Tián and Fúsū commanding them to commit suicide, which surprisingly, they did. This left things open for Húhài to be named as the next emperor.

**05:07** And according to Sīmǎ Qiān, as the royal entourage made its way back to the capital Xiányáng, in order to cover up the stench of the emperor's rotting corpse —

CHINESE SAYINGS BOOK 1
EPISODE 23

this was September — Lǐ Sī had a carriage of dried fish placed before and after the emperor's carriage.

05:27 Then two months later when they got back to Xiányáng, present day Xī'ān, the ruse was continued and no one was the wiser. No one knew the emperor had perished. It was a perfectly executed coup d'état. Then at the most favorable moment for the conspirators, the emperor's death was finally announced.

05:48 Húhài, now Emperor Qín Èrshì 秦二世, before he rowed the Qín Dynasty over the edge of a cliff, he got to enjoy trying out all these imperial powers. He may have been the Qin emperor's son, but he was no Qin Shihuang.

06:03 With this inexperienced malleable 21-year old spoiled boy on the throne, Zhào Gāo was able to quickly assume political control and manipulate the levers of power. Qín Èrshì was happy just to hang in the palace and sample all his deceased father's perks and let Zhào Gāo run the empire.

06:25 Zhào Gāo, while the emperor was busy having fun, began to consolidate his control over the levers of government. Any would-be autocrat with two or more brain cells, in Zhào Gāo's shoes, looking to assume dictatorial powers, knows you gotta suppress all dissenters. Anyone who isn't standing with you is against you. And they gotta go.

06:48 And so we get to the part of the story where this chengyu comes from. Once Zhào Gāo felt confident he had everything at the palace under control, he decided one day to bring a deer to a meeting with the emperor and all the top palace officials. He displayed the deer in front of all those assembled and offered it to the emperor as tribute. Except he didn't call it a deer. He said it was a horse.

07:14  Everyone in attendance on that day knew that wasn't a horse. It was some species of deer. A Lù. It wasn't even a member of the Genus *Equus*.

07:25  The officials all started mumbling and looking at each other. They didn't know what to make of this. This animal standing before them was a deer. But this snake Zhào Gāo, he was declaring his gift to the emperor to be a horse. Even the emperor, at first knew it wasn't a horse.

07:43  Zhào Gāo asked the officials all standing around, pointing at to this hoofed mammal. Is it a deer or horse? Some quick-witted officials twigged on what was going on here. Zhào Gāo was up to something and if they knew what was good for them, they better hop on that train and call that deer a horse. Furthermore, seeing how some of his officials were concurring with Zhào Gāo, the emperor too, he agreed, that was a horse indeed. He always went along with whatever Zhào Gāo said.

08:15  But some officials, they remained silent, or flat out denied this animal was a horse. They insisted, anyone could see, it was a deer. Zhào Gāo expected this and had pre-arranged to have any dissenters summarily

CHINESE SAYINGS BOOK 1
EPISODE 23

executed. He didn't wan't anyone left standing who exhibited behavior that might one day pose a challenge him by pointing to facts or the truth.

**08:41** So anything that involves deliberate misrepresentation of the facts and the distortion of reality, this is what Zhǐ Lù Wéi Mǎ means. Point to a deer and call it a horse. The rest is simple. All those who agree, that's your base. Those who disagree or call you a liar, now you know who's against you.

**09:04** Now you don't have to go to the extremes Zhao Gao went and start murdering or incarcerating people. This chengyu is often used by people to lampoon politicians or companies or charlatans who deliberately deceive by making these grossly false claims.

**09:22** Zhào Gāo back in the late 3rd century BC wasn't the last person to wield political power who used this strategy to smoke out his enemies. Other autocrats have also used Zhao Gao's strategy to eliminate their enemies. But in its more benign form it's a saying you can use to describe anyone who tried to convince you about something by making some utterly false claim.

**09:48** This is a variation to the Hans Christian Anderson folk-tale about the Emperor's New Clothes. Everyone complimented the emperor's new clothes. No one had the courage to tell him the truth, that he had no clothes on. The possible repercussions for speaking the truth were too deadly and perilous. And people, being people and all, valued their lives.

## CHINESE SAYINGS BOOK 1
## EPISODE 23

**10:10** And just in case you're wondering. Later on, after the Zhǐ Lù Wéi Mǎ incident, Húhài, the hapless second Qín emperor, as soon as he started to have regrets about putting so much faith in Zhào Gāo, he ended up being forced to commit suicide. Even Zhào Gāo's co-conspirator Lǐ Sī, that giant of legalism, creator of the small seal script, he too had to go one day. Zhào Gāo had him chopped in half.

**10:39** When the walls finally started tumbling down and the Qín Empire was wracked with revolts and uprisings, Zhào Gāo put Fúsū's son on the throne who we remember as Zǐyīng. And once this grandson of the mighty Qin Shihuang became emperor, he went and did the right thing and had Zhào Gāo killed. And for good measure, he had Zhao Gao's whole family exterminated.

**11:03** Zhǐ Lù Wéi Mǎ. Point to a deer and call it a horse. The secret weapon of any authoritarian regime. Works every time, for a while anyway. But you don't have to be a dictator to Zhǐ Lù Wéi Mǎ. This one is free to use by anyone who is taking the truth, or facts, and purposely misrepresenting them to make their point and get you to believe in their false claims.

**11:29** So, there it is.

**11:47** Until the next time, mesdames et monsieurs, this is Laszlo Montgomery signing off as always from the City of Night here in the State of Confusion. Do think about coming back next time won't you, for another amusing and entertaining episode of the Chinese Sayings Podcast.

 Chinese Sayings Book 1
Episode 24

## LOOKS GOOD ON PAPER

纸上谈兵—Zhǐ Shàng Tán Bīng

This week's Chinese Saying is a well-worn one brought to us by none other than Sima Qian, the Grand Historian. Featured in this story are Lian Po, Zhao She, Zhao Kuo, Bai Qi and the whole Battle of Changping. This is the story of Zhǐ shàng Tán bīng 紙上談兵, a useful chengyu for all kinds of occasions where the end result doesn't necessarily go according to the carefully crafted plan.

## TRANSCRIPT

00:00 | Welcome back everyone, Laszlo Montgomery here with another Chinese Saying. Many of you took one look at this and nodded your heads knowingly and sagaciously because this one is so well-known and has been repeated so many times over the past two thousand years.

00:17 | Zhǐ Shàng Tán Bīng, another well-worn staple that has applications for all kinds of daily life situations. But before we open up The Good Book from whence it came, let's put these four characters on the dissecting table.

00:33 | Zhǐ Shàng Tán Bīng.

Zhǐ Shàng means on paper.

# CHINESE SAYINGS BOOK 1
# EPISODE 24

To tán means to talk or discuss and bīng means weapons, a soldier, an army or just military affairs in general. And in the game of chess, your pawn is called a bīng.

**00:54** Zhǐ Shàng Tán Bīng. This one you don't have to be Albert Einstein or Stephen Hawking to figure out its meaning. On paper discuss military. Right away, we know where this one is heading. But it's not enough just to figure out what this means. This one has a heck of a story attached to it. And without any further wasting of time, let's get down on it.

**01:16** This one comes from that greatest of all founts of useful and interesting chengyu's The Record of the Grand Historian, the Shǐjì. And for today's story we welcome back to the CSP the great Warring States general from Zhào State, Lián Pō 廉颇, featured before in a couple past CSP episodes. Who can forget his incredible display of contrition from the season 3 episode 2, Fù Jīng Qǐng Zuì?

**01:44** From the chapter of the Grand Historian's Shǐ Jì entitled Lián Pō Lìn Xiàngrú Lièzhuàn 廉颇蔺相如列传 The Chronicles of Lián Pō and Lìn Xiàngrú, we get this masterpiece.

**01:56** When this slice of history occurred there were seven remaining states, all warring against each other.

**02:04** And one of these seven warring states was The State of Zhào, created during the 5th century BC during the historic Partition of Jìn 三家分晋. Zhao today could be overlaid on top of Shānxī, Shǎnxī, Héběi and Inner

CHINESE SAYINGS BOOK 1
EPISODE 24

Mongolia. The ancient Chinese heartland.

02:23   The Warring States period in China, roughly 475-221 BC, witnessed the final centuries of the Zhōu Dynasty.

02:32   In the kingdom or state of Zhào 赵, there was a general named Zhào Shē 赵奢, who, along with Lián Pō 廉颇, were known for their many heroic deeds on the battlefield. Zhào Shē had a son named Zhào Kuò 赵括. Like Homer Lea featured in China History Podcast episode 298, Zhào Kuò was enamored with the idea of battle and spent all his days reading and studying about military strategies.

03:00   He liked nothing more than to discuss war with his father's visitors. In these talks, he displayed such thorough knowledge of military history that all the visitors, military men themselves, were greatly impressed and often sang his praises to his father.

03:17   And because Zhào Kuò received so much praise, and so often too, he began to believe all the shoe shining and this made him overconfident and led Zhào Kuò to often act too big for his breeches.

03:31   And his father, General Zhào Shē, he kind of looked at his boy with a degree of disdain. A man like Zhào Shē was a grizzled veteran of too much slaughter on the battlefield. He knew what it was like to fight a battle. And he would tell his son, Zhào Kuò, not to speak so pugnaciously and to exercise more caution and to think more practically. He would tell his son that engaging an

CHINESE SAYINGS BOOK 1
EPISODE 24

enemy on the battlefield wasn't as simple as what he yammered on about in front of people.

04:01 When Zhào Shē's wife asked him why he wasn't proud of his son, Zhào Shē replied, 'War is a serious matter that affects the fortunes of an entire country. One must treat war with gravity and careful consideration. But our son treats it like a game. Nothing good will come of it.'

04:21 In 262 BC, trouble struck the State of Zhào. The Qín army, led by the famously ruthless general Bái Qǐ 白起, invaded the Zhào Kingdom's neighbor, Hán. They surrounded a prefecture in the Hán Kingdom called Shàngdǎng 上党 and were able to cut it off from the Hán capital. The Hán generals based in Shàngdǎng found themselves surrounded by the Qín army and immediately sent emissaries to the Kingdom of Zhào to plead for help.

04:51 Though he'd live to regret it, the King of Zhào stepped up for his ally in Hán and ordered two hundred thousand troops, under the great General Lián Pō, to engage the Qín army. Lián Pō's troops encamped at nearby Chángpíng 长平, and a Qín army division led by Wáng Hé 王齕 hurried to engage him in battle.

05:13 Lián Pō, with his decades of battle experience, had concluded that the best way to defeat the Qín army was to hold Chángpíng. Chángpíng, today is a two and a half hour drive north from Luòyáng. It was easy to defend and difficult to attack, and Lián Pō believed that the Qín army, by battering itself continually against the Zhào defenses

CHINESE SAYINGS BOOK 1
EPISODE 24

hunkered down on Chángpíng, would eventually wear itself out and become weakened to the extent that they'd either give up or be left open for attack.

05:47   This strategy caused the Qín army considerable difficulty. They were far from their Shǎnxī home and their supply lines were growing too thin. It became more and more impossible to supply the Qín troops besieging Chángpíng. Meanwhile, Lián Pō stubbornly held onto the town with a vice-like grip, easily fending off Qín attacks.

06:11   After three years from 262 to 260 BC, the Qin military besieged Chángpíng at considerable expense to themselves. But in all this time they had achieved little. The Qín troops found themselves at the end of their tether and reluctantly reported their dire situation to King Zhāoxiāng of Qín.

06:32   King Zhāoxiāng asked for advice from his strategist Fàn Jū 范雎. And Fàn Jū advised, "The main thing is to get rid of General Lián Pō. He is too cunning and experienced for us to really stand a chance. If our generals can eliminate him, the rest will be easy."

06:51   So spies from the Qín Kingdom were sent to infiltrate Zhào. After insinuating themselves into Zhao society, they began to bribe any officials and ministers they met. After buying their loyalties with gold, these Zhào turncoats became shills for the Qín and gladly spread all kinds of misinformation and rumours at the Zhào court.

**07:15** They said to the King of Zhào, 'Look at Sleepy General Lián Pō, old and timid, being besieged by the Qín army without doing anything about it. It's been three years already and he hasn't made any headway. I fear your majesty, any day now, Lián Pō's army will fall to the Qín!'

**07:35** Then they whispered to the King, "Remember how faithfully and victoriously General Zhào Shē led our armies? Such a great warrior he was. Well, we have heard, your majesty, that he has a son, Zhào Kuò, even braver and more talented than his father. If this Zhào Kuò were to be appointed general at Chángpíng, the Qín army would truly stand no chance!

**08:01** The King of Zhào was already getting impatient with Lián Pō's strategy of rope-a-dope defense. It seemed like the Zhào army at Chángpíng was only reacting to the Qín's offense, never acting proactively themselves. So, with these rumours being constantly whispered in his ear, the King of Zhào immediately sent messengers to Zhào Kuò, ordering him to take over command of the Zhào army at Chángpíng.

**08:27** By this time, Zhào Kuò's father, General Zhào Shē, had passed away. Zhào Kuò's mother, remembering Zhào Shē's words about his son, begged the king not to let her son go to Chángpíng. She repeated Zhào Shē's belief that, even though Zhào Kuò was well-read in military strategies, he treated war like a game, and moreover was too arrogant and confident in his own abilities. 'If you let him lead an army, he will lead us to defeat! she pleaded

CHINESE SAYINGS BOOK 1
EPISODE 24

with the king.

08:58  But the King of Zhào, filled with all the disinformation of these Qín shills, was dead set on replacing Lián Pō with Zhào Kuò. Seeing that she could not dissuade him, Zhào Kuò's mother had to settle for extracting a promise from the King that in the event that Zhào Kuò went down in defeat, the king would not punish any other members of the Zhào clan.

09:23  And with this ringing endorsement from his own mother, Zhào Kuò set off with an additional two hundred thousand troops to the Zhào camp at Chángpíng.

09:33  Combined with the two hundred thousand already at Chángpíng, Zhào Kuò was in command of four hundred thousand Zhào troops. After relieving Lián Pō of his command, Zhào Kuò immediately switched tack from Lián Pō's defensive strategy. He gave orders to counterattack each time the Qín army tried to engage them in battle. He ordered them not to act in a purely defensive position. The Zhào were to fight them and give chase rather than simply defending the Zhào encampment.

10:06  Meanwhile, the Qín army was undergoing its own change in leadership. King Zhāoxiāng's brilliant strategist Fàn Jū, hearing that his plan had worked and that Lián Pō had been replaced with Zhào Kuò, gave orders that the Qín ever-victorious general Bái Qǐ, who had captured and held Shàngdǎng from the Hán Kingdom, head to Chángpíng to engage the Zhào army.

# CHINESE SAYINGS BOOK 1
# EPISODE 24

**10:32** Led by Bái Qǐ, the Qín army faked a few assaults on the Zhào camp using a decoy battalion. When these assaults were beaten back, under Zhào Kuò's orders, the entire Zhào army gave chase. These decoy Qín troops led the Zhào army deep within the territory they controlled. Meanwhile, another Qín force of twenty-five thousand special troops cut off the Zhào retreat and then came five thousand Qín cavalrymen charging right at the Zhào army, splitting it in half.

**11:05** Only then did Zhào Kuò realize he had been tricked into abandoning Lián Pǒ's strategy of securing the encampment at Chángpíng. Zhào Kuò ordered his troops to encamp where they were. But their new position was terribly disadvantageous and badly exposed. They were surrounded on all sides by the Qín army, divided from each other, and their supply lines, which had been secure at Chángpíng, were cut off in this new position.

**11:34** After forty days of camping in this new position, with no supplies and besieged on all sides, the Zhào army became severely demoralized. Zhào Kuò, after studying his maps and seeking wisdom from past military conflicts, decided to lead one last desperate attempt to break the Qín siege. But by this time, his army was weak from hunger and there were no more reinforcement troops to send from the Kingdom of Zhào.

**12:04** In his last desperate charge out of the Zhào camp, Zhào Kuò himself was shot dead by Qín arrows. Seeing that their general had been killed in action, the entire Zhào army threw down their weapons and surrendered

CHINESE SAYINGS BOOK 1
EPISODE 24

en masse to Qín. Thus, four hundred thousand Zhào troops fell victim to the ruthless general Bái Qǐ at the famous Battle of Chángpíng. The outcome of this battle irreversibly weakened Zhào and gave a huge boost to Qín. And in less than forty years, the Qin would become the unifiers of all of China and their king, Yíng Zhèng would rule as China's first emperor.

12:47 So, Zhǐshàng tán bīng. Nobody knew how to fight a war like Zhào Kuò when he was hunched over a map and surrounded by books. He could show you on paper how to win this battle or that war. But when faced with a real-life situation, he found there was a stark difference between planning it all on paper and dealing with all the randomness that life threw at him. So we can use this idiom for anything, and anything that looks great on paper. But the outcome, who knows, maybe not as simple as what was discussed inside the Pentagon or Russian Defense Ministry.

13:24 And not just in war. In business, politics, and planning of any sort. If the stakes are high and all you've done is put together a plan on paper, that's no guarantee that the outcome will be as you expected it to be. You never know what other variables or random events are lurking out there to foil your best laid plans, so meticulously put together by some public or private brain trust. Zhǐshàng Tánbīng.

13:51 So you can keep this one folded up inside your wallet or cellphone case, if it has any compartments. That's how useful this one is. Even though you are saying

CHINESE SAYINGS BOOK 1
EPISODE 24

Zhǐshàng tánbīng, that doesn't necessarily mean to discuss military strategy. Back when I was in the Made in China consumer products business, my boss and I would always discuss our bīngfǎ for when we were sitting in front of that Costco buyer, trying to get that sale. So Zhǐshàng tánbīng works fine in any situation where you have to plan, scheme or strategize.

14:25 Okay, that's it for this time. Go listen to the multi-part series from the China History Podcast that looks at the Rise and Fall of the Qin for more about this fabled and magnificent time in ancient Chinese history. That series was recently given a makeover. So if you already heard it, give it another listen.

14:47 Okay, time is money. Sorry to keep you for so long. But the Battle of Chángpíng and all, I'm sure you found it all worthwhile. This is Laszlo Montgomery, signing off from drought-stricken LA, goading you as I always do to come back again next time for another didactic episode of the Chinese Sayings Podcast.

# Chinese Sayings Book 1
# Episode 25

## PUTTING OUT THE FIRE WITH GASOLINE

抱薪救火—Bào Xīn Jiù Huǒ

Once again, Warring States heavy, Han Feizi, pulls through for us with an excellent chengyu in this Season 6 closer. Bào Xīn Jiù Huǒ 抱薪救火. Sometimes you think you're helping, but all you're doing is making things worse. Our story goes back to the early 3rd century BC rivalry between Qin and Wei. During the reign of pugnacious King Zhaoxiang of Qin, Wei State had to figure out how to survive this ambitious and energized rival kingdom. The King of Wei's advisors offered conflicting advice about how to help the situation. The king finds out later what was supposed to help his state's situation only made things worse.

## TRANSCRIPT

| | |
|---|---|
| 00:00 | Greetings one and all. Laszlo Montgomery here with another Chinese Saying for your personal collection. Man, did these twenty weeks ever fly by or what? Seems like only yesterday we were pointing at that mulberry tree and scolding the locust tree. This is the tenth and final episode for Season 6. |
| 00:20 | And to finish off the season, for our closer, I pulled a good one out of the hat of useful Warring States Period chengyu's, Bào xīn jiù huǒ 抱薪救火. |

## CHINESE SAYINGS BOOK 1
## EPISODE 25

**00:30** And for the third time in CSP history, we are featuring that superstar of Legalism, Hán Fēizǐ. You can also find today's chengyu not mentioned in the Records of the Grand Historian as well as Romance of the Three Kingdoms, chapter forty-three.

**00:47** But before we jump into the story, let's do the usual character-by-character breakdown and see if you can guess its meaning.

Bào means to hold or carry in your arms, to embrace or hug.

And Xīn means firewood or fuel.

Jiù means to rescue or save.

And huǒ means fire.

**01:10** And when you line all four characters up in a row, you get Carry firewood save fire.

**01:17** Not such an obvious meaning. And like it is with every Chinese Saying, there's gotta be a story behind it that brings those four characters to life.

**01:25** And the story went like this. Towards the end of the Warring States period, the Kingdom of Qín 秦国 was growing in power every day. Its borders were expanding swiftly due to its famous policy of yuǎn jiāo jìn gōng 远交近攻, or attacking its near neighbors while making alliances with those further away. This strategy was

CHINESE SAYINGS BOOK 1
EPISODE 25

introduced to the pugnacious Qin King Zhāoxiāng by his loyal and wise minister Fàn Jū 范雎.

**01:57** One of Qín's main targets for attack was its neighbor, the Kingdom of Wèi 魏国. Between 276 and 274 BC, Qín mounted three invasions of the Kingdom of Wèi, occupying large swathes of Wèi territory and causing no end to the death and destruction they inflicted on the once all-powerful Kingdom of Wèi.

**02:21** In 273 B.C., the Kingdom of Qín launched its fourth attack on Wèi. By this time, morale in Wèi was so low that many soldiers didn't even bother to pick up their weapons against the onslaught. Again, Wèi suffered a devastating loss of territory to Qín.

**02:38** The King of Wèi gathered around his advisors and asked for their advice in creating a strategy against the Qín. An esteemed advisor, Duàngān Zǐ 段干子, suggested that the King of Wèi should voluntarily cede Nányáng 南阳 to the Qín. Duàngān Zǐ said that Nányáng was a prime piece of land and would no doubt please the King of Qín and this good faith gesture would offer King Zhāoxiāng ample incentive to stop attacking Wèi.

**03:09** A visiting politician named Sū Dài 苏代, heard Duàngān Zǐ's suggestion and shook his head. He pointed out to the King of Wèi that giving an inch of territory to the Qín would only demand a mile. He went on to explain that the Kingdom of Qín had clear ambitions to rule all of China, and would not stop until the Kingdom of Wèi was soundly defeated, once and for all.

## CHINESE SAYINGS BOOK 1
## EPISODE 25

**03:34** Some within Wèi were highly suspicious of this strategy proposed by Duàngān Zǐ. Some believed he was purposely suggesting this strategy to weaken the state in order to soften it up so that he, himself could seize the throne.

**03:49** Sū Dài continued: 'Your Majesty, giving this territory to the Qín will be about as effective in quenching their thirst for power, as carrying a bundle of firewood in order to quench a fire.

**04:02** That's right. Here is where Sū Dài compared Duàngān Zǐ's thinking to Bào Xīn, carrying a bundle of firewood to, Jiù Huǒ, to put out a fire. He furthermore advised the King, as long as there is still wood to consume, that fire will never stop burning.' In other words, don't trust Qín.'

**04:28** Despite this convincing argument from Sū Dài, the King of Wèi ended up taking Duàngān Zǐ's advice. He ceded Nányáng to the Qín in hopes that this would appease King Zhāoxiāng and convince him to stop attacking Wèi.

**04:44** But we all know our Qín history and indeed, just as Sū Dài had predicted, the Kingdom of Qín was by no means satisfied with just Nányáng. In the three or four decades that followed, they constantly harried and attacked the Kingdom of Wèi. And when the King of Wèi died, they saw the perfect moment to seize twenty towns from Wèi before a new King could be crowned.

CHINESE SAYINGS BOOK 1
EPISODE 25

05:09 | It all came to an end in 225 B.C. That year, the Kingdom of Qín mounted an all-out siege on the capital of Wèi at Dàliáng 大梁, today's Kāifēng in Hénán province.

05:25 | And in order to defeat Wèi, what they ended up doing was diverting the Yellow River and other nearby rivers so that the capital of Wèi was flooded for three days and irreparable damage was done to the city walls. Once this was accomplished, the armies of Qín poured into the capital, and after a one hundred seventy-eight year history, the State of Wèi finally fell to the Kingdom of Qín.

05:53 | So this Chinese saying Bào Xīn Jiù Huǒ, you can use it for just about any kind of life situation where you think you're trying to help but all you're doing is making things worse. You're adding fuel to the fire, not putting it out. Bào Xīn Jiù Huǒ. As good a saying as there ever was to close out this sixth season of a podcast show many told me wouldn't last more than one or two seasons tops.

06:21 | Bào Xīn Jiù Huǒ, carrying firewood to put out a fire. Sometimes you just wanna lend a hand but all you do it take matters from bad to worse.

06:32 | And until that time, when we meet again on the avenue, this here's Laszlo Montgomery signing off from, where am I, Santa Monica California, just for the day. Take care, my erudite and good looking listeners, and I'll see you in the not-too-distant future for another season and another exciting episode of the Chinese Sayings Podcast.

# Chinese Sayings Book 1
# Episode 26

## THE TRANSCRIPTS

## WHAT'S THE RUSH?

揠苗助长—Yà Miáo Zhù Zhǎng

Laszlo once refers to "The Mengzi" for this short tale of the foolish farmer who wasn't satisfied with nature's pace. This time we look at 揠苗助长 Yà Miáo Zhù Zhǎng. Let's face it, some things in life take time, especially when the natural order of things is involved. This farmer back in the ancient state of Song thought he had developed a winning technique to speed the growth of his fields. It didn't turn out as he expected.

## TRANSCRIPT

00:00 | Good evening once again all CSP listeners and lovers of Chinese chéngyǔ's, Laszlo Montgomery here with the Chinese Sayings Podcast, bringing you a quickie this time. I'll have you on your way in no time at all.

00:13 | Quick though this episode may be, it has a 24-karat provenance and comes to us direct from The Mèngzǐ or the Mencius as it's also known. Zhū Xī, the great Neo-Confucian philosopher grouped the Mengzi into the Four Books, the Sì Shū of Confucianism, the most essential of philosophical works.

00:35 | And from the chapter titled Gōngsūn Chǒu 公孙丑 comes

CHINESE SAYINGS BOOK 1
EPISODE 26

this gem. Gōngsūn Chǒu was one of Mèngzǐ's disciples. This Confucian classic book is a feast of dialogs, anecdotes, references from history and a number of blue chip chengyu's.

01:00 And our Chinese Saying for this time is Yà Miáo Zhù Zhǎng.

Let's break this one down like we always do.

Yà Miáo Zhù Zhǎng.

To Yà something means to pull up or to tug with an upwards motion. Now, in some versions of this saying the character Yà is replaced with bá 拔 which means basically the same thing. When you bácǎo 拔草, you're pulling weeds. But for this episode, I hope no one has any objection to sticking with the character Yà.

And a miáo is a young plant or a seedling or a sprout.

Zhù means to help or to assist.

And the last character Zhǎng, when used as a verb, means to grow or develop.

01:48 Yà Miáo Zhù Zhǎng, pull sprout assist grow. You might be able to catch a whiff of what these four characters mean. But once again, when you know the backstory, everything makes a lot more sense.

02:02 So we open up the Mèngzǐ to the section where he is

CHINESE SAYINGS BOOK 1
EPISODE 26

having a conversation with his disciple Gōngsūn Chǒu.

02:10   And the Second Sage, as Mèngzǐ was also called, Confucius being the Great Sage of course, told Gōngsūn Chǒu about this farmer from the kingdom of Sòng. Sòng had its capital in Shāngqiū, Henan province, right near the border with Shandong. Confucius's father came from Song and ended up in Lǔ State, in case you were interested.

02:32   Mengzi told of this farmer there who was stressing out something terrible over the seeds he had planted in his field. Every day when he went out to work in his fields he kept wringing his hands about how slowly the sprouts seemed to be growing. He kept thinking they should have been a certain height by now but from the looks of things, something needed to be done to put things right.

02:57   So one morning, he went out into the field, bent down and began ever-so-gently pulling on each individual seedling. He Yàmiáo, he tugged on that sprout. And after spending the whole day in his field, he observed the results of his efforts to zhùzhǎng or assist in their growth, and, feeling satisfied that they appeared taller, he gathered up his things and returned home.

03:26   After this hard day's work, over dinner, this farmer proudly boasted to his family how tired he was after such an exhausting day. He went on to explain how nature seemed to not be working fast enough. And because of that, he had, one by one, yàmiáo, tugged on

CHINESE SAYINGS BOOK 1
EPISODE 26

the sprouts in order to zhù zhǎng assist the seedlings in their growth

03:50   The farmer's eldest son, knowing his dad like he did, excused himself from the table to go out to the fields to see what his father hath wrought. And fearing the worst he found a whole field of seedlings, each one partially uprooted and already starting to shrivel and wilt away, beyond salvation. With feeling a grave disappointment, he saw that his father had gone and Yà Miáo Zhù Zhǎng.

04:21   And as Mèngzǐ explained to his disciple Gōngsūn Chǒu, there are few men who do not wish for their efforts to come to fruition as quickly as possible. Those who give up on their labours as too much hard work are just like lazy farmers who do not weed their fields.

04:39   On the other hand, those who are too aggressive and anxious to see results ASAP are just like that simple-minded farmer from Sòng who pulled his seedlings out of the ground in his attempt to speed their growth. Not only did that not help, it ended up hindering his harvest.

04:58   Yà Miáo Zhù Zhǎng. To pull a seedling to aid its growth. This one's used for any kind of life situation to describe someone who is so impatient to grow or to succeed that in attempting to see quicker results they end up taking actions that ultimately make them worse off than they were before.

05:20   A common example often cited to go along with this chengyu are the Tiger parents who exhaust their child

CHINESE SAYINGS BOOK 1
EPISODE 26

by sending them to these bǔxíbān cram schools, while simultaneously enroll them in sports, music classes and other preparatory classes, making plans to enroll their kids in Harvard or Peking U while they're still in first grade. They, too, have been described as Yà Miáo Zhù Zhǎng.

05:47  So, no matter in your own family, in business, in agriculture or in anything, sometimes when you Yà Miáo Zhù Zhǎng, you try and do whatever you can to push things along so that the gratification can come that much faster. But all you're doing is tugging on those sprouts to help them grow. You're not letting nature take its course. By going against nature and pushing things too fast, you end up doing some damage instead. Follow Mengzi's advice. Don't do it.

06:18  And kids too. Some children are in such a hurry to grow up. In elementary school they're already trying to be teenagers. And teenagers become too anxious to become grown-ups. Through their actions they attempt to push the laws of nature to their limit. Remember, as we say in English, Slow and Steady wins the race. Yībù Yībù baby!! Often times there're no short cuts in life.

06:47  All right, that's all I got for you for this time. Mèngzǐ. He believed in the innate goodness of human nature. His mother wanted the best for him but you didn't see Mèngmǔ attempting to Yà Miáo Zhù Zhǎng. And perhaps because of that everything turned out just fine for her little Mèng Kē 孟轲.

## CHINESE SAYINGS BOOK 1
## EPISODE 26

**07:03** | OK, just like I promised, nice and quick, the way these CSP episodes were meant to be. I thank you all for stopping by and listening. This is Laszlo Montgomery signing off from the same recording studios used by the CHP in wonderful Los Angeles California. And I'm entreating you to come back again next time for another exciting episode of the Chinese Sayings Podcast.

# Chinese Sayings Book 1
# Episode 27

## MIRROR, MIRROR ON THE WALL

门庭若市—Mén Tíng Ruò Shì

We wander back to the 4th century BC to the State of Qi under its great King Wei. There was a handsome resident of Qi named Zou Ji who had a thing about a certain Mr. Xu. From Zou Ji's obsessive concern about his good looks compared to Mr. Xu, it ultimately leads to a fateful meeting with the King of Qi. And from this meeting and the results that followed we get the Chinese Saying 门庭若市 Mén Tíng Ruò Shì. Why was the King of Wei's palace courtyard compared to a crowded marketplace? Listen to the amusing story behind this chengyu and find out.

## TRANSCRIPT

00:00 | Hey everyone, Laszlo Montgomery again. This is the Chinese Sayings Podcast and do I ever have a good one for you.

00:09 | Mén Tíng Ruò Shì, a chengyu that comes straight out of the Zhànguó Cè, the Annals of the Warring States. It was written during the Western Han so it's pretty reliable. The Warring States period of the Eastern Zhōu lasted 490 to 221 BC, roughly the passing of Confucius to the unification of China by Qín Shǐhuáng. The Western Han was established in 202 BC so the Annals of the Warring States is a pretty reliable record, filled with colorful

# CHINESE SAYINGS BOOK 1
# EPISODE 27

anecdotes, mainly concerning political strategy.

**00:43** But before we get to the story, let's break Mén Tíng Ruò Shì down into its constituent parts.

A Mén is a door or an entrance, and a Tíng is a front courtyard or front yard.

Ruò means as if, or like.

And the final character shì means a market or a marketplace. It also means a city, but in this case it means market.

**01:10** Door-courtyard as if a market. I think we can make a sound educated guess about the meaning behind these four characters. But let's not leave ourselves guessing and go find out for sure. The tale behind Mén Tíng Ruò Shì takes place in the State of Qí during the time of their great King Wēi, Qí Wēi Wáng. He ruled from 356 to 320 BC and was the first ruler of this powerful state to call himself a king rather than a duke or some other title.

**01:45** You all might recall Qí, located in Shāndōng province, was the last of the warring states to fall to Qín. King Wēi of Qí reigned concurrently with Duke Xiào of Qín. All fans of the Qín Empire, Dà Qín Dìguó miniseries know Duke Xiào was the ruler who recruited Shāng Yāng to the Qín side.

**02:09** Anyway, the star of our tale was one heck of a shuàigē 帅哥. The Zhànguó Cè, the Annals of the Warring States

190

CHINESE SAYINGS BOOK 1
EPISODE 27

refers to our hero as a Měi Nánzǐ, a beautiful man. Let's just say, he was handsome. And his name was Zōu Jì 邹忌. And he came from Qí State.

**02:29** One day, as Zōu Jì was checking himself out in the mirror, liking what he saw, as always, he knew he turned heads around town. But he couldn't help obsessing about this one other good looking guy named Mr. Xú, Xú Gōng. He himself had heard folks around town often remarking on Mr. Xu's dapper good looks. And as Zōu Jì gazed at his reflection, he wondered, who was more attractive and handsome, himself or Mr. Xú 徐公.

**02:59** He went to his wife and asked, "Dear, who do you think is better-looking, me or Mr. Xú?" His wife replied without hesitation, 'Mr. Xú? Oh, he's nothing compared to you. Nobody in their right mind would ever choose Xú Gōng over you?'

**03:16** But his wife's endorsement wasn't enough for Zōu Jì. He next went to his concubine and asked the same question, to which she replied timidly, "How can Mr. Xú hope to compare with you? You're much better-looking"

**03:28** The next day, Zōu Jì, he still had these nagging doubts. He had a friend over for dinner. Over the meal, Zōu Jì put the same question to his companion. His friend, who happened to need Zōu Jì's help with something, replied with a smile, 'Lǎo Zōu, you are much more attractive man than Mr. Xú.'

**03:51** Although his wife, concubine, and friend had all told him that he was far more handsome than Mr. Xú, Zōu Jì didn't entirely believe them, and remained suspicious of their remarks.

04:02 As it happened, the next day, Mr. Xú himself came to visit, and Zōu Jì had the chance to really get a good look at him. As they sat together chatting, Zōu Jì studied every square inch of Mr. Xu's face and couldn't help but feel this Mr. Xú was far more handsome than he was.

04:22 After Mr. Xú left, Zōu Jì went to the mirror and once again surveyed himself thoroughly, comparing every feature of his body with what was fresh in his mind from this encounter with Mr. Xú. The more he thought about it, the more certain he became that Mr. Xú was by far the better-looking of the two. And he was not happy.

04:42 That night, Zōu Jì could not sleep. His mind kept returning to the same question: If Mr. Xú was clearly more handsome, why had three people told Zōu Jì otherwise? After much contemplation, fulmination and reflection, it dawned on Zōu Jì: his wife had told him he was more handsome because she was biased towards him; his concubine had told him he was the more attractive one because she was afraid of him; and his friend had told him he was more handsome because he knew he wanted something from him.

05:18 From this incident, Zōu Jì drew a profound conclusion: if a nobody like him received all this flattery, imagine what if must be like for the ruler of a country. He would be surrounded by even more flatterers than himself, and

CHINESE SAYINGS BOOK 1
EPISODE 27

thus was even more vulnerable to false counsel.

05:37　The very next day, Zōu Jì went to the Qí court in Línzī 临淄 and told his story to King Wēi of Qí. He concluded his time with King Wēi by imploring him, for the good of the state, to place more value on the criticisms from his officials and from the people and to pay less heed to the endless stream of compliments from all these flatterers who secretly wanted something from him.

06:01　King Wēi saw the value of Zōu Jì's words and promptly issued a decree: "From this day forth, he who dares to criticize my actions to my face will be rewarded highly; he who dares to criticize my actions via letter will be rewarded moderately; he who criticizes me behind my back, but whose opinion reaches my ears, will receive a small reward. And these measures shall apply no matter whether the dissenter is a commoner or a courtier."

06:34　After this incident, so many people, commoners and courtiers alike, ran to the Qí royal court to issue their criticisms, King Wēi's gates and courts became as crowded as a market on market-day. That's right, right here in the Zhànguó Cè states that so crowded was the entrance to the royal palace with people wishing to petition or criticize the king, the Mén Tíng, the courtyard to the entryway, was Ruò Shì, like a marketplace, which are usually quite bustling.

07:07　And just as a follow-up to this story, as the chapter covering Qí State from the Annals of the Warring States goes, so many people came forward to express

# CHINESE SAYINGS BOOK 1
# EPISODE 27

their criticisms and complaints to King Wēi. And so valid were many of the criticisms, they were taken into consideration by the Qí court and implemented throughout the land.

07:30 Because of this, the crowds became smaller and smaller month by month. After a year, not a single complainant could be found at the palace gates. Because King Wēi had implemented so many of these reforms with such great success, there was nothing left that anyone could point to that needed reforming.

07:49 Under King Wēi's wise and humble rule, the Kingdom of Qí grew in prosperity and strength day by day. Emissaries from far and wide came to pay their respects: the Kingdoms of Yān, Zhào, Hán, and Wèi all sent representatives. Because of this incident, King Wēi of Qí was remembered in history as a ruler who scored victories without even using force.

08:16 Mén Tíng Ruò Shì. Literally, doors and courtyards like a marketplace. You can use this to describe any situation where there are an abundance of guests or visitors to a place.

08:33 Oh, and one more thing, remember Lord Mèngcháng 孟尝君 from Season 1, Episode 7, Jī Míng Gǒu Dào, well, King Wēi was his grandfather. Just sayin'. Lord Mèngcháng, he was the one with the huge entourage.

08:47 Okay, enough of this factoids. I doubt that one will ever make its way to Jeopardy.

CHINESE SAYINGS BOOK 1
EPISODE 27

**08:51** Let's wind things up here. Mén Tíng Ruò Shì. When some places are so crowded that nobody goes there anymore, this is a good one to use. Mén Tíng Ruò Shì. Keep that one in your utility belt. You never know.

**09:05** Thanks everyone for listening. This is Laszlo Montgomery signing off from Los Angeles, California. Hey, come visit June-July 2026. We got the World Cup coming to our fair city. That is not a paid endorsement from FIFA. Take care everyone and I look forward to speaking with you again next time for another enlightening episode of the Chinese Sayings Podcast.

 Chinese Sayings Book 1
Episode 28

## LOCKED AND LOADED

厉兵秣马—Lì Bīng Mò Mǎ

Here comes one more textbook chéngyǔ from the Spring and Autumn Period, as written by Master Zuo Qiuming 左丘明 himself. 厉兵秣马 Lì Bīng Mò Mǎ. Lots of marquee names from that exciting time, including Duke Mu of Qin and Duke Wen of Jin. Be sure to check the website for a handy downloadable cheat sheet listing all the Chinese names and terms. This one has a fair number of characters and place names. The kind of inter-kingdom rivalries that were one of the hallmarks of the Eastern Zhou are front and center in this 7th-Century BC tale. This is a good Chinese Saying that has a few useful applications in real life.

## TRANSCRIPT

00:00 | Welcome all Chengyu lovers across the universe to the Chinese Sayings Podcast. Laszlo Montgomery here with another jewel in the crown of great Chinese Sayings from the Zuǒ Zhuàn, The Commentaries of Zuǒ, written sometime during the 4th century B.C. Master Zuǒ Qiūmíng's 左丘明 scholarly musings on the Spring and Autumn Annals.

00:23 | Today's chengyu, Lì Bīng Mò Mǎ, comes to us from the chapter titled Xī Gōng sānshísānnián 僖公三十三年 that stated: "Zhèng Mù Gōng shǐ shì kè guǎn, zé shù zài lì

| | bīng mò mǎ yǐ" "郑穆公使视客馆，则束载厉兵秣马矣 |
|---|---|
| 00:41 | And before we get to this great 7th century BC story, let's break these four characters down.<br><br>Lì Bīng Mò Mǎ.<br><br>The first character Lì, in its archaic usage means to grind or to sharpen.<br><br>Bīng means weapons, arms or a soldier.<br><br>Mò as a verb means to feed horses. As a noun it means fodder.<br><br>And a Mǎ is horse. Horses make it into a lot of chengyu's. |
| 01:13 | Lì Bīng Mò Mǎ, Sharpen Weapons feed horses. Doesn't sound like this one is destined to be a love story. |
| 01:20 | It all went back to the 620's BC. Duke Wén of Jìn, also remembered as Chóng'ěr 重耳 and Duke Mù of Qín 秦穆公, these two stars of the Spring and Autumn Period of the Zhou Dynasty collaborated on a takedown of Zhèng State. But before they united to destroy Zhèng, an emissary was sent to Duke Mù of Qín from Zhèng warning him, if he let Jìn take Zhèng, that was gonna be bad for Qín and would only strengthen Jìn at Qín's expense. |
| 01:54 | So Duke Mù withdrew his army and told Duke Wén he was backing out of the whole thing. But Duke Mu left |

CHINESE SAYINGS BOOK 1
EPISODE 28

behind a garrison just outside of the Zheng and kept and continued to keep eye on things there. And the one left in charge to command this Qín garrison was named Qǐzǐ 杞子.

02:13 | A couple years later, in the winter of 628 BC, Qǐzǐ sent word back to Qín, saying he was now in possession of the key to the Zhèng capital's north gate. And Qǐzǐ further said if you send troops now they could easily mount an ambush on the capital and that would be the end of Zhèng.

02:35 | When Duke Mù of Qín received this message, he was overjoyed and immediately designated three of his most capable generals, Mèng Míngshì 孟明视, Xī Qǐshù 西乞术, and Bái Yǐbǐng 白乙丙, to lead an assault on Zhèng.

02:48 | But his advisor Jiǎn Shū 蹇叔 warned Duke Mù, this whole thing had danger written all over it and was a rash undertaking. He went on to explain that a thousand lǐ of open land existed between Qin and the Zhèng capital in present day Huázhōu 华州, a district of Wèinán, Shǎnxī. And most of that distance ran through the territory of the Kingdom of Jìn. Jiǎn Shū pleaded with Duke Mù, How are you going to march all these thousands of troops such a long distance, through Jìn territory no less, and keep the affair secret? And then what happens if the troops are discovered? We'd be at the mercy of Jìn or Zhèng.

03:27 | But Duke Mù was convinced, an opportunity such as this, to attack Zhèng will never pass this way again. He pointed out to Jiǎn Shù that the risk of attack from

Jìn was very low, since, in 627 BC Duke Wén of Jìn had just passed away and the new Duke Xiāng 晋襄公 had more important things to deal with. Therefore, Duke Mù refused to heed Jiǎn Shū's advice and signed off on the idea of ambushing the Zhèng capital.

03:58 It just so happened that Jiǎn Shū's son was enlisted into this special unit of elite soldiers sent to ambush Zhèng. On the day the soldiers were to depart, Jiǎn Shū followed them all the way to the city's east gate, weeping. He called out to his son: 'If you are ambushed in Jìn, as I have no doubt you will be, you can be sure that I will travel there to ensure a proper burial for you.'

04:25 Duke Mù heard about this and was absolutely livid at Jiǎn Shū and demanded, why'd you have to go and say all that! But Jiǎn Shū already knew how this whole campaign was gonna end and that he'd never see his son alive again.

04:42 After a terrible journey, the army of Qín finally arrived at the Kingdom of Huá 滑国 on Zhèng's borders. Today's Suī County 河南睢县, about an hour west of Shāngqiū 商丘. Huá was a minuscule state that was a fiefdom of the royal Zhou Family.

04:59 As luck would have it, a Zhèng merchant named Xián Gāo 弦高 was selling goods in Huá. And you can imagine his utter astonishment at seeing a whole army of Qín soldiers.

05:11 But Xián Gāo thought fast on his feet and hid his surprise well. He approached them and began making small talk was quickly able to discover what they were up to.

CHINESE SAYINGS BOOK 1
EPISODE 28

05:21 | Knowing that Zhèng was wholly unprepared to take on a surprise attack from the Qín army, and filled with patriotism for his home state of Zhèng, Xián Gāo immediately dispatched a messenger to alert the Duke Mù of Zhèng of these troop deployments down in tiny Huá State. Qin and Zheng States at this time in 627 BC, both had rulers named Duke Mù.

05:47 | Meanwhile, the clever Zhèng merchant Xián Gāo disguised himself as an ambassador from Zhèng and approached the Qín generals with gifts of cattle and cattle hides and said, as if he had been waiting for them all this time, 'My lords, Duke Mù of Zhèng, has heard of your approach and welcomes you and sends you these cattle as a gift for your soldiers after such a long journey.'

06:11 | This ruse had the desired effect of tricking the Qín generals into thinking that Zhèng already knew everything about their ambush plans. Faced with this unexpected turn of events, the Qín generals began to consider a Plan B which caused them to linger further in Huá. This bought time for the messenger to deliver his missive to Duke Mù of Zhèng.

06:35 | As for Qīzǐ, the Qín general who had first alerted Duke Mù of Qín that he had the key to the north gate and it was possible to breach the capital, he had calculated the exact number of days it shoulda taken the invading Qín force to rendezvous with him outside the capital. Thinking they'd be arriving imminently at his garrison post, Qīzǐ called for his men to Lì Bīng, begin sharpening their

**07:12** weapons and to take particular care in Mò Mǎ, feeding their war horses, so as to be ready for action at any minute. While this was going on, the merchant Xián Gāo's messenger arrived at the Zheng court and was able to warn Duke Mù of everything Xián Gāo had told him. The Duke of Zhèng sprang into action and called for his people to immediately make preparations for war. He also sent spies to check on the Qín garrison, to see whether they really were preparing for attack.

**07:36** When the Duke of Zhèng's spies saw the preparations for war going on inside the Qín barracks, and that they were in the midst of Lì Bīng Mò Mǎ, they knew that Xián Gāo's warning was true beyond a doubt. Before Qīzǐ was ready for battle, Zhèng soldiers immediately surrounded the Qín barracks. Seeing this, Qīzǐ guessed that the secret was out. Thinking that Zhèng had turned the tables on them, he gave the orders to the Qín troops to skedaddle and they quickly abandoned the garrison and beat a retreat and somehow they managed to escape.

**08:13** And in order to avoid being accused of having started the whole thing, Duke Mu of Zheng ordered his hastily assembled army to not do anything further or try to prevent Qīzǐ's soldiers from escaping.

**08:26** They turned heel and returned to Zhèng. When Qīzǐ, in full retreat, ran into the incoming Qín generals, he told them to turn around and that someone had blabbed to Zheng and they were all in position there lying in wait for Qín to fall into their trap. And Qīzǐ advised the best course of action was to forget about the mission and hightail it

CHINESE SAYINGS BOOK 1
EPISODE 28

08:52   back to Qín. Somehow, Zheng knew everything.

But, just as Jiǎn Shū had warned Duke Mù of Qín, on the march back to Qín, they were ambushed by Jìn forces as they passed through the Xiáo Mountains of Western Hénán. And at this Xiáo Zhī Zhàn 殽之战 or Battle of Xiáo, the Qín forces were wiped out and the three generals, Mèng Míngshì, Xī Qǐshù, and Bái Yǐbǐng, were all taken as prisoners of war.

09:17   And as a result of this whole sorry incident and the Battle of Xiáo in April 627 BC, Jìn State grew more powerful and became the most feared of all Eastern Zhou states. As for Qin, they took a big hit and this defeat slowed them down for many years. They focused their efforts against the nomadic tribesmen to their west instead and bided their time, growing in strength.

09:45   And one more thing, Duke Xiāng of Jìn was convinced by one of his people to release the three generals and allow them to return to Qín where they would surely be executed. So the three generals were released and they returned to Qín. And wouldn't you know it, when they arrived on the Qín border, there was Duke Mù himself, dressed in white mourning clothes, wailing and crying out that this whole thing was all his fault and he should have listened to the correct advice of his advisor Jiǎn Shū. The three defeated generals were not punished.

10:19   So the chengyu Lì Bīng Mò Mǎ means to sharpen the weapons and feed the horses. It describes the action of preparing for battle. But it can also be more commonly used as a metaphor for making full preparations in advance. And you don't have to invade a country to use the Chinese Saying of Lì Bīng Mò Mǎ. In business, when you're going into a meeting where multi-million dollar contracts are at stake and when your deal team is prepping for this you can also say you're Lì Bīng Mò Mǎ.

10:52 Any kind of situation where you really have to do your homework and make sure you are all set to take on any kind of monumental task or mission, first you have to Lì Bīng Mò Mǎ.

11:06 Nothing can be left to chance. There's no such thing as being too prepared.

11:10 So sharpen the weapons and feed the horses. Lì Bīng Mò Mǎ. The good old Chronicles of Zuǒ, a veritable goldmine of chengyu's.

11:20 OK, I shan't keep you any further. I know you have bigger and better podcasts to listen to. This is Laszlo Montgomery signing off from snowy Los Angeles, hoping you enjoy the audition and that you'll come back next time for another exciting episode of the Chinese Sayings Podcast.

 Chinese Sayings Book 1
Episode 29

## I SHOULD HAVE KNOWN BETTER

借箸代筹—Jiè Zhù Dài Chóu

This time around we're reaching all the way back to those fateful years following the fall of the Qin Dynasty and the contentious period of conflict between Liu Bang of Han and Xiang Yu of Chu. As these two rivals battle it out, Liu Bang sought advice from one of his advisors on a plan of action. But as we'll see, that plan is blown out of the water by the great hero of the early Han, Zhang Liang. In order to persuade Liu Bang of the folly of this plan, Zhang Liang will 借箸代筹 Jiè Zhù Dài Chóu, borrow chopsticks to illustrate his strategy. And using these chopsticks as a prop to illustrate his point, Zhang Liang blows this advisor's good idea out of the water.

## TRANSCRIPT

00:00 | Hey everyone, Laszlo Montgomery with you once again. This is The Chinese Sayings Podcast.

00:06 | As some of you may have noticed, you can now get this program not only on the Chinese Sayings Podcast feed, but also on the China History Podcast feed. And what I found out is that despite all my milquetoast efforts at spreading the word about this show, not to mention these Chinese Sayings podcast shows being available since 2017 fleet-wide on Cathay Pacific, still, this labor of love, has been relegated to a niche inside of a well-

# CHINESE SAYINGS BOOK 1
## EPISODE 29

hidden room that very few seem to know about.

**06:37** But not anymore. It's moving up in the world, and the CSP is now being made available, simultaneously on the China History Podcast feed. And why not? Every single one of these Chinese sayings are rooted in history that we've already covered to some extent or another in previous CHP episodes.

**00:54** So give it a shot and see if you like them. They're all quite short. And no one ever said learning a new chengyu or Chinese Saying was gonna hurt anyone.

**01:04** And this time we're going to give Jiè Zhù Dài Chóu a once-over and see how this term, to borrow chopsticks to make a plan on someone's behalf, came about.

**01:14** Like a healthy share of these Chinese Sayings, this one comes to us from Sima Qian's Records of the Grand Historian from the chapter 留侯世家 Liú Hóu Shì Jiā. The Family of Liú Hóu. Marquis Liú was one of the honorary titles given to one of the dramatis personae of our chengyu for this time.

**01:31** But before we dive in, let's break these four characters down and see what we got to work with this time.

Jiè Zhù Dài Chóu.

To Jiè something is to borrow or lend or in this example, to make use of.

CHINESE SAYINGS BOOK 1
EPISODE 29

Zhù is another word for chopsticks.

Jièzhù, borrow chopsticks.

And Dài means to take the place of or substitute.

Last character Chóu means to prepare or plan. It also means strategy as a noun as well as a chip, a gambling chip.

02:05 So Jiè Zhù Dài Chóu. Borrow or make use of chopsticks to Dài chóu, take the place of strategy.

02:13 Today's story from Sīmǎ Qiān is straight out of the Chǔ-Hàn Contention, the Chǔ Hàn Zhànzhēng 楚汉战争. That's right, the epic battle between Xiàng Yǔ 项羽 and Liú Bāng following the fall of the Qín Dynasty. These two larger-than-life figures from the late 3rd Century BC battled for supremacy to become the new emperor of China, just like Yíng Zhèng did back in 221 BC when he founded the Qín Dynasty.

02:41 In 204 BC, the Chǔ general Xiàng Yǔ had the Hàn general Liú Bāng trapped in Xíngyáng 荥阳, today's western Zhèngzhōu. Liú Bāng was obsessive about wanting to vanquish Chǔ King Xiàng Yǔ. Even during mealtimes, Liú Bāng gathered his men together and discussed their next moves and their strategy after that.

03:05 And it was during one of these mealtime conferences that Liú Bāng called upon one of his ministers, a Confucianist of note, named Lì Yìjī 郦食其 to proffer his

## CHINESE SAYINGS BOOK 1
## EPISODE 29

ideas for what was to be done with Xiàng Yǔ.

**03:15** Lì Yìjī advised: To solve this matter we should look to the past for guidance. 'You recall back when the Xià Dynasty was defeated, the new Shāng dynasty king granted feudal territories to the descendants of Xià. And when the Shāng dynasty was displaced in its turn, the new King Wǔ of Zhōu granted territories to the descendants of Shāng. And after that, everything was fine.

**03:40** 'But times have changed since those days from centuries ago. The situation now is thus: the Qín Dynasty, who preceded us, lacked any understanding of honour and custom, and abandoned the concept of ruling by moral guidance and virtuous principle, embracing legalism instead.

**03:59** 'Thus, when the Qín was established, it granted no concessions to the former nobility of those kingdoms it conquered. Now, if you were to vow to remedy this situation by granting territories to the six warring states destroyed by the Qín, this would gain you great goodwill in all those lands.

**04:18** And the nobility and common folk of those former kingdoms would see that you, Liu Bang, King of Hàn, are a benevolent ruler and they will therefore follow you willingly. Then you will be able to face Xiàng Yǔ and his Southern armies as a Hegemon of the North. By then, Xiàng Yǔ will have no choice but to surrender to your superior rule.'

CHINESE SAYINGS BOOK 1
EPISODE 29

04:40 | Líu Bāng sat silent and thought about this plan. And then, feeling satisfied, Líu Bāng at once ordered seals to be carved decreeing his concession of territories to the nobles of each of the six kingdoms that had been absorbed by the Qin Dynasty.

04:57 | But before Lì Yìjī could rise from the dinner table, in came another advisor named Zhāng Liáng 张良. Zhāng Liáng's council had been useful before, so Líu Bāng turned to Zhāng Liáng and recounted Lì Yìjī's strategy to him, and asked his trusted advisor his opinion.

05:14 | Zhāng Liáng immediately exclaimed: 'Whose idea was this? If you adopt this plan, you are doomed.'

05:20 | Líu Bāng was taken aback and you could hear the murmuring in the room amongst all the most senior Hàn military men. Why is that, Liu Bang asked?

05:30 | Zhāng Liáng replied, 'I'll be better able to tell you if you will let me use the chopsticks on the table to illustrate my point.'

05:39 | Yes, it's right here, early in the story that Zhāng Liáng mentions the four characters, when he tells his king he will Jiè Zhù Dài Chóu. He was going to use these chopsticks on the table to make his point.

05:55 | And grabbing all the chopsticks in his fist, Zhāng Liáng began to explain. 'First of all, in the past, when King Tāng of Shāng set the precedent of granting territories to the descendants of the conquered dynasty, he had already cornered Xià into such a position that their demise was certain.

06:11 'Are your Hàn forces in such a position that Chǔ's demise is imminent?" Do you see Xiàng Yǔ giving up or weakening?'

06:20 Líu Bāng was forced to admit that his army enjoyed no such position. And this contention between himself and Xiàng Yǔ was far from over.

06:28 Zhāng Liáng threw down a single chopstick on the table and said, "Well, that is the first reason you cannot adopt this plan.

06:37 'Secondly, what Lì Yìjī says about King Wǔ of Zhōu granting fiefdoms to the descendants of Shāng is very true. But by the time King Wu gave away those territories, his capture and subsequent execution of his enemy, the last King of Shāng, King Zhòu 商纣王, was all but certain. Can you say the same about your opponent, Xiàng Yǔ ?'

07:01 Líu Bāng again admitted that he could not.

07:05 Zhāng Liáng threw down a second chopstick and said, 'And that is another reason this plan will surely fail. Thirdly, when King Wǔ of Zhōu conquered the capital of Shāng, he restored order to the ravaged city immediately. He had posters made proclaiming the new order; he had the tombs of the Shāng kings refurbished; and he set free the Shāng princes he had captured during battle. Do

CHINESE SAYINGS BOOK 1
EPISODE 29

you have the resources to restore order to the cities that you will have to destroy in order to defeat Xiàng Yǔ in battle?'

07:37 Again, Líu Bāng said that he did not.

07:41 Zhāng Liáng threw down a third chopstick and said, 'And that is a third reason this plan is no good. After the fighting to overthrow the Shāng Dynasty had ended, King Wǔ distributed grain from his own granaries and silver from his own treasuries to assuage the sufferings of the peasants. Do you have King Wǔ's deep pockets that will allow you to placate the common folk following your victory?'

08:02 Once again, Líu Bāng had to admit his situation was far from equal to King Wǔ's back in the 11th century BC.

08:11 Zhāng Liáng threw down a fourth chopstick and said, 'And that is a fourth reason you cannot go ahead with this. When King Wǔ of Zhōu conquered Shāng, he had all his war chariots converted to carts for everyday transport; he had his army's weapons put away and stored upside down, and threw tiger-skin cloth over the arms to signify that he had no intention of using them again.

08:37 'Now, when you give away your territories to the former Warring States nobles, can you make the same promise that you'll never disturb the peace again?'

08:44 Líu Bāng said that he could not.

## CHINESE SAYINGS BOOK 1
## EPISODE 29

**08:48** Zhāng Liáng threw down a fifth chopstick and said, 'And that's a fifth reason you cannot give away your territories now. When he had conquered Shāng, King Wǔ of Zhōu pastured his war horses south of the Hua Mountain, to show that he had no more use for them. Once you've distributed these lands, can you set your war horses to pasture?'

**09:09** Líu Bāng admitted he would always need them to be battle-ready all the time.

**09:14** Zhāng Liáng threw down a sixth chopstick and said, 'And that is a sixth reason you should not distribute lands to the former lords. After he had pastured his war horses, King Wǔ of Zhōu also pastured his transport oxen north of Taolin, to show that no longer would he be using them to supply armies. Can you also make this gesture of peace?'

**09:37** Líu Bāng was silent. There was no need to say that he could not do what King Wǔ did.

**09:44** Zhāng Liáng threw down a seventh chopstick and said, 'And that's a seventh reason you cannot go forth with this plan. Now, last but not least, these former lords of the six defeated warring states have abandoned their ancestral lands and bid goodbye to their friends and family to join your army, all in hopes that if you win against Xiàng Yǔ of Chǔ, you might one day grant them a feudal territory. If you were to grant them that territory now, before you have gained victory, they will take their soldiers, throw down their arms, and return to

CHINESE SAYINGS BOOK 1
EPISODE 29

their own lands. Their loyalty to you has no roots. And after they've secured territory of their own through your graciousness, they are free to transfer their support to Xiàng Yǔ if they wish. What can you do about it? Then where will you get your allies who will help you in your campaign against Chǔ?'

10:35   Saying this, he threw down the eighth chopstick.

10:40   Staring down at eight chopsticks' worth of good reasons on the table before him, Líu Bāng spat out the food in his mouth and cursed Lì Yìjī, saying, 'You useless bookworm! If I had listened to the impractical advice you gave me, my affairs would be ruined!' And immediately, he sent people to retrieve the seals he had ordered sent out to the six former lords. They were brought back and destroyed.

11:05   And ever since The Grand Historian's mention of this vignette from Chinese history, these words Jiè Zhù Dài Chóu are used in sentences to describe the action of helping someone else strategize or come up with a plan. Sometimes they will just say Jiè Zhù 借箸, borrow chopsticks to mention the act of helping someone strategize with whatever the perplexing problem is.

11:31   But if someone you know is trying to think up a strategy or course of action to take and they don't know what to do, you can step in and Jiè Zhù Dài Chóu. You don't have to actually use chopsticks to dramatize your point. By uttering these words from two thousand and more years ago your aims are clear. You're just trying to help

## CHINESE SAYINGS BOOK 1
## EPISODE 29

|       | someone strategize what to do. |
|-------|--------------------------------|
| 11:55 | Okay, this was a long story, but like it is with all these chengyu's, having this info stored in your random access memory might come in handy one day. |
| 12:05 | Okay, thanks for listening everyone, if you made it this far. This is Laszlo Montgomery signing off from rainy LA, and thank god for that. Please do consider coming back again next time, for another exciting episode of the Chinese Sayings Podcast. |

 Chinese Sayings Book 1
Episode 30

## WOULDN'T CHANGE A THING

一字千金—Yī Zì Qiān Jīn

Here is another well-known and useful chengyu. In this episode, we examine the 3rd century BC story behind Yī Zì Qiān Jīn (一字千金). This is the one that came to us direct from The Grand Historian Himself and it features Lü Buwei, Lady Zhao, and the father of the future first emperor of China, King Zhuangxiang. This is one of the classic stories from the Qin State.

## TRANSCRIPT

| 00:00 | Welcome back again everyone to another season of the Chinese Sayings Podcast. Laszlo Montgomery here with the Season 8 opener and did I ever pick out a good one for you. |

| 00:10 | Back in 1979 when I began studying Chinese, the teacher told us about these sì zì chéngyǔ, four character chengyu or idioms. How could I have known back then what she was talking about. She explained it like slang expressions that only had four characters. It took one or two more years of Chinese study before I started to learn more about these chengyu phrases and that while most of them were four characters, some were five, six, or more characters, depending on the story. |

# CHINESE SAYINGS BOOK 1
# EPISODE 30

**00:42** When I first got started with my self-study of these Chinese Sayings, I did so with a book I purchased in Taipei, probably at Caves Books, during the summer of 1980. I bought this book called Měi Rì Yī Cí 每日一词 which means A Word a Day. And the very first story in this book that I studied character by character is the chengyu for today, Yī Zì Qiān Jīn.

**01:11** And the story behind this saying is one of the most repeated tales from all of ancient Chinese history. It comes to us straight from the Records of the Grand Historian and concerns the story of Master Lǚ Bùwěi.

**01:22** And when you hear that name, it's a given that the story behind today's Chinese Saying Yī Zì Qiān Jīn, concerns the life of China's first emperor, Qín Shǐhuáng or as he was known before then, Yíng Zhèng.

**01:37** Before we re-tell this great story from the chapter of the Record of the Grand Historian called Lǚ Bùwěi lièzhuàn, 吕不韦列传 The biography of Lǚ Bùwěi, let's first review the four characters behind Yī Zì Qiān Jīn.

Yī means the number one and a Zì is a Chinese character.

Qiān means a thousand.

And Jīn means gold.

**02:03** Real simple, this one is, One character a thousand gold. And for the backstory behind these four syllables that don't appear to mean anything, let's get right into the

CHINESE SAYINGS BOOK 1
EPISODE 30

02:14 story.

At the end of the Warring States period, in a relatively insignificant state called Wèi 卫国, there lived a wealthy merchant named Lǚ Bùwěi. This was the state of Wèi in northeast Henan that is usually spelled W-E-Y to differentiate it from the more consequential and way more powerful and much bigger state of Wèi. Same sound, different Chinese character.

02:40 Lǚ Bùwěi was a rich merchant who often went on business trips to Hándān, the capital of Zhào state. On one of these trips, purely by happenstance he made the acquaintance of a prince of Qín state named Yíng Yìrén 嬴异人.

02:56 In the state of Qín, Yìrén was not an important personage. His father, King Xiàowén of Qín, had more than twenty children by various concubines, and Yìrén was somewhere in the middle in the order of succession. So his father had sent him to the state of Zhào as a political hostage.

03:17 Yìrén's new friend Lǚ Bùwěi, he was one heck of an ambitious man. He wasn't satisfied with only being rich and successful. That wasn't enough for him. He was also hungry for power and working in the palace. And as soon as he met the acquaintance of the son of the King of Qín, he immediately saw an entree into politics in the form of Yíng Yìrén.

03:41 Lǚ was thinking. If he could somehow get Yìrén selected as the heir to the state of Qín, which was now one of the most powerful of the Warring States, then he himself could ride on Yìrén's coattails to power. With this in mind, Lǚ Bùwěi began to make every effort to deepen his friendship with Yìrén. First off, he made all his wealth available to the prince. He even gave Yìrén one of his own favourite concubines named Lady Zhào or Zhào Jī 赵姬. By displaying all this extravagance and performing these favors, Lǚ Bùwěi soon became Yìrén's most trusted and influential advisor.

**04:25** With Lǚ Bùwěi's sponsorship, encouragement, and adeptness at scheming, Yìrén was indeed able to position himself as the heir to the Qín throne. And in November of the year 250 BC, indeed, Yíng Yìrén ascended the throne as King Zhuāngxiāng of Qín 秦庄襄王.

**04:45** Lǚ Bùwěi could hardly believe his good fortune. King Zhuāngxiāng named him his chief advisor, and granted Lǚ rich lands around the city of Luòyáng in Hénán. But unfortunately for King Zhuāngxiāng, he wasn't able to enjoy being in the top spot for long. Barely three years after he ascended the throne, in 247 BC he passed away. His thirteen-year-old son by Lady Zhào, Yíng Zhèng, was named the next king of Qín.

**05:17** Despite the loss of his Ticket to Ride, so to speak, Lǚ Bùwěi was able to turn this situation to his advantage as well. He had Yíng Zhèng, who was after all only a thirteen-year-old boy, acknowledge him as his adoptive father, and named him regent. Thus, the ultimate power of the Qín state now rested with Lǚ Bùwěi and his former

CHINESE SAYINGS BOOK 1
EPISODE 30

concubine, Lady Zhào, Zhào Jī.

05:45 Oh, and by the way, Lǚ Bùwěi, despite fixing Lady Zhao up with the late King Zhuangxiang, he never gave up his own intimate relationship with Concubine Zhào and in fact, the Grand Historian sorta intimates that Yíng Zhèng... well, his father may not have been King Zhuāngxiāng, if you get what I mean.

06:08 As regent, Lǚ Bùwěi realized that the other powerful states of the Warring States period, Zhào (赵), Chǔ (楚), Qí (齐), and Wèi (魏), each had famous scholars and great schools, and were thus academically renowned and admired throughout the land. Lǚ Bùwěi was frustrated that Qín, although it had become a military powerhouse, was still a relative nobody when it came to famous works of literature or schools of thought. All the great works and scholarly academies were all to the east of Qín.

06:44 Thus, one of the first uses to which he put his great wealth and power as regent of Qín was to attract talent to Qín, offering them the best of treatment and the most comfortable of tenures if they would come to Xiányáng, today the city of Xī'ān. Many scholars found this offer irresistible, and soon Lǚ Bùwěi had more than three thousand scholars under his name.

07:11 These scholars came from diverse schools of thought and each had unique specialties, strengths, and viewpoints. As advisors as well as a source of cultural prestige, they became an invaluable political resource for Lǚ Bùwěi.

# CHINESE SAYINGS BOOK 1
# EPISODE 30

**07:26** To show off his new pool of scholars, Lǚ Bùwěi had them, according to each of their own strengths, write a series of more than a hundred and sixty essays on the many events of the Spring and Autumn period that had preceded the Warring States period of the present times. These essays ranged widely across disciplines, comprising essays on geology, astrology, geography, politics, history, and more.

**07:56** What had been produced represented the greatest compendium of knowledge that was available to scholars in China at the time.

**08:05** In 239 BC, these essays were all compiled into one great book that has survived down to our day and it's called *Master Lǚ's Spring and Autumn Annals* 吕氏春秋, the Lǚshì Chūnqiú.

**08:18** Even back then, understandably, he was extremely proud of this book. He had the entire thing carved onto the largest bamboo strips available, and posted all hundred thousand or so characters onto the city gates of the Qín capital of Xiányáng.

**08:34** Above it, he had someone hang a notice that said something to this effect: "If a scholar from any part of China can improve this work by adding or deleting even a single character, I will reward them with a thousand *liáng* of gold." A liáng is fifty grams. 1.8 oz to my fellow Amerykanskis scratching their heads.

**09:00** Then as a further enticement, just like they do in Vegas,

CHINESE SAYINGS BOOK 1
EPISODE 30

displaying a million bucks under guarded plexiglass, the thousand *liáng* of gold was put on display beside the bamboo strips on which the book had been written. Add or delete a single character to improve this work. Who could do it?

09:21 Well, don't forget the 3rd century BC times they lived in. No one, not a single scholar dared to proffer any suggestions that would alter *Master Lǚ's Spring and Autumn Annals* in any way. This was admittedly a great work, as all China literary scholars will agree today. And look at how many chengyu's the Lǔshì Chūnqiú has yielded throughout the ages. A couple made it to this educational program. This is the third one.

09:49 The literary folk of Xiányáng, and there were quite a few, they knew it was already a great work. But frankly speaking, no one dared challenge the likes of chancellor Lǚ Bùwěi, whose backstory and egotism was well known to all.

10:04 And now in our day and I'm sure all throughout Chinese history, this chengyu is good to use for any kind of literary work where you want to remark that the content, as written, was perfect. So masterfully written, not even the smallest edit was necessary. You can actually mean it, if you feel that way. Or it's a handy idiom to use when you wanna shoeshine your colleague or some literary figure, journalist that you meet, oh this was just perfect Yī Zì Qiān Jīn. I wouldn't even change a word.

10:40 So, there you haves it. Don't forget this Chinese Sayings

# CHINESE SAYINGS BOOK 1
# EPISODE 30

Podcast is also available in the China History Podcast feed. I see most of you have been checking it out.

**10:55** And my great thanks to all of you, my wonderful CHP CSP community all over the world, this is Laszlo Montgomery signing off from Los Angeles at the beginning of what's shaping up so far to be a hot town, summer in the city. I welcome you to come back once more with feeling, for another exciting episode of the Chinese Sayings Podcast.

www.ingramcontent.com/pod-product-compliance
Lightning Source LLC
LaVergne TN
LVHW061610070526
838199LV00078B/7229